Translated from the Russian by Yuri S. Shirokov

Published and distributed throughout the world by T.F.H. Publications, Inc.

T.F.H. PUBLICATIONS, INC.
211 West Sylvania Avenue
Neptune, NJ 07753

Distributed in the UNITED STATES by T.F.H. Publications, Inc., 211 West Sylvania Avenue, Neptune City, NJ 07753; in CANADA to the Pet Trade by H & L Pet Supplies Inc., 27 Kingston Crescent, Kitchener, Ontario N2B 2T6; Rolf C. Hagen Ltd., 3225 Sartelon Street, Montreal 382 Quebec; in CANADA to the Book Trade by Macmillan of Canada (A Division of Canada Publishing Corporation), 164 Commander Boulevard, Agincourt, Ontario M1S 3C7; in ENGLAND by T.F.H. Publications Limited, 4 Kier Park, Ascot, Berkshire SL5 7DS; in AUSTRALIA AND THE SOUTH PACIFIC by T.F.H. (Australia) Pty. Ltd., Box 149, Brookvale 2100 N.S.W., Australia; in NEW ZEALAND by Ross Haines & Son, Ltd., 18 Monmouth Street, Grey Lynn, Auckland 2 New Zealand; in SINGAPORE AND MALAYSIA by MPH Distributors (S) Pte., Ltd., 601 Sims Drive, #03/07/21, Singapore 1438; in the PHILIPPINES by Bio-Research, 5 Lippay Street, San Lorenzo Village, Makati Rizal; in SOUTH AFRICA by Multipet Pty. Ltd., 30 Turners Avenue, Durban 4001. Published by T.F.H. Publications Inc. Manufactured in the United States of America by T.F.H. Publications, Inc.

THE OFFICIAL BOLSHOI BALLET BOOK OF
SWAN LAKE

Yuri Grigorovich and Alexander Demidov
Photography by Vladimir Pcholkin

Scene from the Swan Lake
on opening night, 1877.

**Captions for all the photographs were written by
Dr. Herbert R. Axelrod**

The exterior of the Bolshoi Hall in Moscow.

In order to understand the story of Swan Lake, and the meaning of the various dances and scenes, begin reading only the captions to the photographs which start on page 85.

CONTENTS

Above: Maya Plisetskaya as Odette. Facing Page: Nata-
lya Bessmertnova as Odette and Alexander Bogatyryov
as the Prince.

Gallery of Interpreters

ODETTE

Polina Karpakova.
1877.

Anna Sobeshchanskaya.
1877.

Lyubov Roslavleva.
1901.

Adelina Dzhuri.
1901.

Valentina Kudryavtseva.
1925.

Lyubov Bank. 1928.

Nina Podgoretskaya. 1928.

Sofia Golovkina.
1937.

ODILE

Rimma Karelskaya.
1953.

Nina Timofeyeva.
1956.

Tatyana Golikova.
1971.

Marina Leonova.
1972.

Yekaterina Giltzer.
1903.

Vera Korali.
1910.

Margarita Kandaurova.
1917.

Viktorina Kriger.
1925.

Irina Tikhomirova.
1938.

Mariana Bogolyubskaya.
1942.

Galina Ulanova.
1948.

Raisa Struchkova.
1951.

FOREWORD

Swan Lake is the emblem of Russian ballet. Every Soviet ballet company has it in its repertoire. This work of Tchaikovsky's genius ushered in the history of Russian classical ballet music, and it has played an enormous role in the evolution of the Russian classical school of dance. No other ballet is better known, more popular and more loved in the entire history of world choreography.

However, the music of *Swan Lake* had a difficult destiny, at times unexpected and contradictory. Very much is still unknown about it, and it is full of mystery and challenge. To meet this challenge is a matter of first priority to the Bolshoi Ballet.

It will be recalled that Tchaikovsky composed *Swan Lake* especially for the Bolshoi. This is why it has appeared on the Moscow stage in a variety of choreographic versions.

I came up with my first production of *Swan Lake* in 1969. It is now seventeen years since then, but I am still working on it. In its present choreography *Swan Lake* may be described as the fifth version of my production of 1969.

For all its outward simplicity *Swan Lake* irresistibly attracts the choreographer like a powerful magnet, demanding an answer to its mystery.

In my view *Swan Lake* has an enigma about it that holds the attention of the audience like a crystal ball watched by a crystal gazer. So great is the charm of genuine chefs-d'oeuvre of art created by human genius.

Yuri Grigorovich
Moscow
August, 1986

Supplementary information about the color photographs

An Idea Is Born

1. A New Home

"My dear brothers:

"My journey is over. It was uneventful and cheerless, and all this time I kept thinking of you and wondering if my dreadful melancholy had lately been too much of a bore for you..."

This begins Tchaikovsky's first letter from Moscow to A.I. and M.I. Tchaikovsky. It is dated 6 January, 1866. A stickler for punctuality, he indicated the time of completing the letter: 3:30 p.m.

He had reached a turning point in his life. The years of study at the St. Petersburg Conservatory, the desperate search for recognition, the career of a law officer, the life of a young man of the world pained by the strange duality of his situation and unable to find a way out of it, were now in the past.

Tchaikovsky became a professional musician relatively late in life. "I was made an official no good for his job," he remarked once. Music attracted him irresistibly, but he delayed his decision, uncertain of his fitness for an artistic career. He was haunted by vague dreams mingled with boredom and fits of despair followed by frantic moments of euphoria.

"What is to become of me? What can I expect from the future? — I am terrified to think of that," he wrote in a letter to his sister Alexandra. He was 21 and already sensed the unfairness of destiny that would eventually crush him.

"For the time being, however," he wrote defiantly, "I am seeking nothing but pleasure and enjoying life whatever the cost."

The chilling breath of fate, its stealthy and relentless steps were a theme that in a few years he would translate into the language of music, which alone would offer him a refuge from the vicissitudes of life and the fear of the inevitable.

An artist's rendering of P. I. Tchaikovsky.

That, however, was yet to happen. In the years under review more mundane concerns held his attention: the likelihood of a promotion with a 20-rouble raise in salary, bitter regrets about his weaknesses and carefree life, and eager hopes that no precious time had yet been lost.

His enrollment in the St. Petersburg Conservatory in 1862 was the first sign of a coming change. He studied composition with Anton Rubinstein. Thoughts of his calling as a composer obtruded themselves on his mind. "Sooner or later I'll quit my office job and devote myself to music for good," he told his friends. So far he could not afford it, and he kept his job to earn a living.

Shortly before completing his last term at the St. Petersburg Conservatory he wrote in a letter to his sister: "As I think of my future, I realize with growing clarity that music alone is the right road for me." In 1865, three months upon graduation, he accepted the post of teacher of theory and composition at the Moscow Conservatory.

Tchaikovsky's resettlement in Moscow was a considered step. With his artistic cast of mind he detested the mind-numbing drudgery of government service, so he gave it up without feeling much regret about his ruined career. A new life was beckoning to him. He was now a professional musician in his own right and on his way towards a different and better life of intriguing uncertainty and nebulous, yet fascinating, promise. We have ample reason to describe that step as a romantic flight from the habitual and boring routine of daily existence towards a different destiny in the world of music.

Moscow with its hustle and bustle of a large industrial and commercial city, throbbing public life and atmosphere of traditional Russian hospitality favorably impressed the 25-year-old newcomer. "All strangers look like friends here," he wrote in his first letter from Moscow. That however, was too early to say with assurance. In fact, it had taken some time before he felt really comfortable here. Much of Moscow's life had proved alien at first.

Indeed, Moscow was sharply different from St. Petersburg for its tenor of life, tastes and customs. In his early period here Tchaikovsky recoiled in disgust from some time-honored habits of its privileged classes for all his efforts to conform to convention. The city seemed too "carnal" at first. Here physical enjoyment prevailed over intellectual pursuits, — that was his first impression of local life at any rate, — and he was unable to adapt to it at once.

Moscow's society amazed him with its overindulgence and extravagance, which were a far cry from the austere grandeur, moderation and stiffness of St. Petersburg.

"In Moscow they eat incredibly much and drink to excess without regard for decency, while women here are overly inflammable. Boozing and gluttony are a matter of course here," he wrote in a letter.

Tchaikovsky was a man of subtle tastes and refinement, and his exquisite nature revolted at the sight of this side of Moscow life. It was nauseating to him.

He expressed his resentment with such ugly facts in almost every letter of his first two years in Moscow. That painful conflict with alien life would stir up the romantic element of his genius and add fuel to the antagonism between his inner world of delicate emotions and the hostile world of coarse self-enjoyment and conceit around him.

His disillusionment was a natural state for one of the finest minds of Russian society. The stifling social climate that prevailed at the time generated growing public discontent, which was strikingly manifest in the widespread "Chekhovian sentiments" within the midst of the Russian intelligentsia. Tchaikovsky was not a tough fighter by nature, but his troubled emotions and constant dissatisfaction with the established routine of social existence cried for a vent where he was in his element — in the realm of music.

But, habit cures habit, as the saying goes. He gradually got used to his new surroundings, and nostalgia loosened its grip on his heart. New friendships among intellectuals made him change his mind about the city's life. Eventually, he came to love Moscow almost as dearly as his native St. Petersburg.

Moreover, his twelve years in the city were perhaps the best time of his life. That was a time of stability, not always comfortable and well-organized but eventful enough, with a variety of new acquaintances and, most important of all, his first serious attempts at composition.

His Moscow period culminated in a disastrous wedlock, which entailed another flight, this time into a wonderland of artistic travels, which left no room for hopes for a quiet life in a cosy family circle. Strange as it may seem, there had been no signs of impending catastrophe in the years preceding that escape. True, he had been haunted by some vague forebodings of disaster, but in fact he had invited it himself to see if he could meet that challenge.

His marriage was not a surrender to public convention but a long-planned step, as is evidenced by his own repeated allusions to his desire to join a family, and he spoke of his longing for a married life more and more often as he advanced in years. Another motive was subconscious as much as apparent in the light of his circumstances was his hidden desire to break out of the vicious circle of his new captivity — the captivity of the Moscow Conservatory circles and teaching routine, a life of stability and the monotonous march of time.

Whatever it might be, his marriage hastened his decision to leave Moscow. And who knows, was it not the best thing to happen under the circumstances? Nature denied him the simple comforts of family life but it rewarded him generously with the superior blessing of artistic freedom and an independent life of creation.

Swan Lake was composed at the end of his Moscow period. Its music is pervaded with an almost imperceptible premonition of change, sentimental dreams of happiness, and a fatalistic foreboding of a calamitous storm that would sweep old life away before the final purification of the soul.

This ballet reflects as faithfully as a mirror the various psychological nuances which colored the composer's life in that period: his romantic passion, lyrical meditation and sincerity, as well as quests of happiness and its inevitable and terrible end.

Swan Lake may be the most personal of all the compositions he created in Moscow. One can easily discern in its music a poetic illustration of the composer's own destiny.

The Attitude Towards Ballet in Russia

The amount of various music Tchaikovsky composed during his twelve years in Moscow was fantastically enormous by today's standards. Five operas, four symphonies, large program compositions, about forty lyrical songs — these are but a few of the long list of his works of that period.

He was literally consumed by an insatiable thirst for composing, and he delighted in writing music in all genres, so much so that he seemed at times to be simply unable to hold his ebullient energy in check.

He felt a strong attraction to opera. There were historical reasons for that interest. In the mid-19th century Russian musicians paid keen attention to opera, regarding it as the most important genre in view of its democratic and realistic character. Tchaikovsky shared this view. In his opinion, opera appealed to the massive audiences and brought the composer closer to the people.

"An opera may be performed as often as forty times during a season, while a symphony may be played once in ten years," he used to say. Opera brought the art of music within reach of the common people rather than the select few. Tchaikovsky believed that an operatic composer was motivated by a natural desire to widen the range of this listeners. Opera alone could affirm his reputation as a mature composer and win him genuine success and fame.

Tchaikovsky in 1889.

Initially Tchaikovsky made no serious plans linked with ballet in those years. He was firmly convinced that ballet had no solid basis for existence. That was reasonable to presume at the time. As Yuri Bakhrushin, a notable student of Russian ballet writes, " the largest number of performances a ballet could expect was ten to twelve in a year. In later years this number declined drastically, while a ballet that had survived in the repertory was performed no more than two or three times a year." Besides, a ballet that had dropped out of the current repertory vanished from the stage for good, as a rule.

The public attitude to ballet music in the 1860s and 1870s left much to be desired. Steady ballet goers felt satisfied with music of the standard of Minkus or Pugni, which was mostly incidental to a production, so that serious Russian musicians listed ballet as a second-rate genre. The attitude to ballet as a showy spectacle for entertaining the aristocracy was common among the progressive artistic intelligentsia. Making up his mind to compose *Swan Lake*, therefore, Tchaikovsky was taking a chance.

The Inside Story

The Directorate of Moscow Theaters offered Tchaikovsky a fee of 800 roubles for composing the music for *Swan Lake*. This was a small fortune at the time. That was partly the reason why he accepted the offer. In a letter to Rimsky-Korsakov he frankly admitted that he had agreed to do this work for the sake of money because he was hard up.

Tchaikovsky's attitude to ballet, however, was different from that of many intellectuals of his time, though he could not afford to ignore the consensus within the midst of serious musicians. It was clear that his experiment in the genre of dance music would fail to excite their interest, and he had no illusions on this score from the start.

As is evidenced by Hermann Laroche, his friend and a brilliant music critic, "Tchaikovsky viewed ballet as a genre of art on a par with others." His interest in the fantastic musical drama, which was his idea of ballet, was of a platonic character, so he visualized it probably in general outline without thinking of how it would fit in with his own musical plans."

Laroche recalls further that "Tchaikovsky took a skeptical view of his assurances that as a composer he had a special talent for ballet music."

It is clear from Laroche's reminiscences that Tchaikovsky's attitude to ballet was ambivalent. For all his interest in it he had his doubts about its promise and its fitness to himself as a musician seeking recognition, who had but recently entered upon an independent path in the field of artistic creation. His letter to Rimsky Korsakov illustrates that duality. Admitting his financial motive, he speaks of his long cherished dream of trying his hand at ballet music.

The tone of that letter, however, is cautious, to say the least. In fact, Tchaikovsky felt uncertain of the aims and results of his work as long as he composed *Swan Lake*. He had a dim idea of its future.

To the best of our knowledge, the situation was, indeed, unclear. It would be safe to presume that before getting down to work Tchaikovsky had fairly accurately sized up the creative potential of the Bolshoi ballet troupe as it was in the last century. As is known, he was a knowledgeable ballet lover. As his brother Modest Tchaikovsky testified, he had gained an understanding of the technique of ballet dance from his frequent attendance of ballet performances, so much so that he could appreciate the importance of *balloné, elevation* and *firmness of toe* as much as other intricacies of the art of dance.

In those years the Bolshoi ballet was certainly far below its present excellence. It was, in fact, a provincial troupe in the true sense of the word, which could not even dream of competing against the celebrated ballet of St. Petersburg and had practically no successful productions on its record.

Moreover, the troupe was handicapped by frequent reshuffles of choregraphers, none of whom was gifted enough to lead it to success. Vaclav Reisinger, the first choreographer of *Swan Lake*, had gained a disputable reputation as a ballet master long before its première and was called a "choreographic virtuoso" by his colleagues only in jest.

As for the Bolshoi orchestra, Tchaikovsky had commented on its performance in derisive words even before the production of *Swan Lake*. Incidentally, the orchestra had rehearsed the ballet only twice before its première, so one can only wonder about its standard of playing the music under the baton of S.Y. Ryabov, the conductor, who was a "worthless musician" in Tchaikovsky's phrase.

Worse still, the ballet libretto and program had evidently been prepared with undue haste, without a clearcut plan of work and in an amateurish atmosphere. It is known from the reminiscences of Karl Waltz, an artist and scenographer of the Bolshoi, that Tchaikovsky ran into difficulties caused by the absence of a working relationship with Reisinger. Waltz reminisced that "before composing the ballet Tchaikovsky had long been trying to find whoever could supply him with accurate information on the music required for dance." This is confirmed by the music critic

Nikolai Kashkin, a friend of Tchaikovsky, who writes in his memoirs that the composer "collected ballet scores from the theater's library and studied their composition in detail."

By all indications many person of widely different artistic tastes and professional qualifications took part in compiling the ballet program and libretto. They were so much the product of a collective effort that it is hard to name exactly the librettists of *Swan Lake,* since the involvement of V.P. Begichev and V.F. Geltzer in writing the scenario has long been held in doubt by musicologists, though their names are displayed on the playbills. On the première playbills these names were absent, and their owners have never claimed the authorship of the libretto of *Swan Lake.*

In that situation Tchaikovsky could be confident of only one side of the ballet project: the financial reward for his work on the music. He had known all along that to hope for a brilliant production of *Swan Lake* would be wishful thinking, so he accepted the failure of the première with resignation. According to Modest Tchaikovsky's testimony, "he showed a lukewarm interest in that event very much unlike the nervous tension and excitement he felt at the first-night performances of his operas, so, he was not much disappointed by the production, which was, of course, far from brilliant. The unpicturesque stage scenery and costumes, the absence of first-class dancers, the ballet master's poor imagination and, finally, the orchestra, fairly good in composition but directed by Mr. Ryabov, a worthless musician, who had never dealt with such a complex score before — all these facts put together allowed the composer to blame the failure of the première on others."

Blaming others with or without reason hardly looks like Tchaikovsky's way but his brother's other evidence is plausible. The failure of the ballet was something he had long been prepared for, so it did not come as a surprise. The composer's story of a rehearsal of *Swan Lake,* the only one that has reached us, vividly illustrates his impressions of the work on the production under the guidance of the "choreographic virtuoso" Reisinger. In his letter to Modest Tchaikovsky he says: "Yesterday I watched the first rehearsal of some numbers from the first act in the hall of the theatrical school... You should have seen the ballet master inventing dances to the accompaniment of a lonely violin with an expression of profound wisdom and inspiration on his face. It was a most comical sight. It was just as amusing to watch the dancers of both sexes putting on pleasant smiles intended to humor an imagined audience and visibly enjoying an easy opportunity to jump and whirl, while performing a sacred duty."

This is caustic irony, indeed. Though Tchaikovsky liked the world of ballet, he took it with a grain of salt, and much of what he saw simply amused him.

Karl Waltz recalled that the composer had taken a keen interest in the stage setting of *Swan Lake*, especially that of the final scene in which the heroes died, as they did in the original version, and on his insistence a veritable deluge was arranged on the stage. Waltz writes that this scene "engaged the composer's attention very much."

It may be relevant to say a couple of words about Tchaikovsky's general attitude to ballet and what he valued in this art most of all. To believe Modest Tchaikovsky's testimony, "he was fascinated mainly by the fantastic side, and he did not like ballets devoid of magic transformations and flights." Laroche writes in the same vein that ballet was a "kingdom of dreams, fantasy and magic" necessary to the composer; it was a world where "words or songs did not belong... a pure fairy tale expressed in pantomime, dance and plastic groups."

Therefore, Tchaikovsky attached special significance to the fantastic side of a ballet performance, and he requested Waltz to present a "veritable deluge" on the stage. He wanted *Swan Lake* to be a fairy tale ballet, picturesque and fascinating.

The composer's creative ideas were not limited to the visual effects of ballet. He valued in ballet the organic links between its different components and unmistakably sensed the synthetic nature of the theater. "Music inspired by the plot should in turn inspire the ballet master, the scenographer and the machinist" — that was Laroche's definition of a ballet production Tchaikovsky would regard as ideal. Small wonder, therefore, that the composer praised *Giselle* as the supreme achievement of the art of ballet of his time.

Dissatisfaction With His Own Music

Tchaikovsky's opinion of his music for *Swan Lake* is a matter of guesswork to this day. Nothing definite is known about it, and the scant facts available to us contradict each other too much to suggest a reasonable conclusion.

At the time of composing the ballet, Tchaikovsky never commented on his work, and in his letters of that period he mentions it only casually and very seldom. It is true, some of his remarks in conversations with members of his close circle showed his irritation with the process of composition, but these might have been made on the spur of the moment, since he was a man of moods.

In one of his letters Tchaikovsky speaks of his work on the ballet as "an endlessly boring drudgery." In another letter he mentions it along with complaints about his most onerous duties: writing articles and teaching Conservatory classes. It is easy to guess the reason for his attitude to the ballet. It was a severe time shortage he was to overcome to be able to meet the deadline. He had evidently expected to complete the composition in record time, since, as he thought, a job like that would be a simple task for him. His permanent time trouble, however, forced him to extend his work on *Swan Lake*. In fact, it took him a full year to get it done!

The composer made his first direct comment on the music of *Swan Lake* more than half a year after its première. Having watched the ballet *Sylvia* by Léo Délibes in Vienna at the end of 1877, Tchaikovsky called *Swan Lake* "pure crap" which he recalled with a feeling of shame. We can see this remark twice in his correspondence with his wealthy patroness Mme von Meck and the composer Sergei Taneyev, who was his pupil.

What was the reason for that severe verdict Tchaikovsky passed on his own ballet? Can it be trusted in general?

In that period, which was the end of 1877, new features emerged in Tchaikovsky's music, and he took a stern critical view of almost all his compositions created in Moscow. In the period between the première of *Swan Lake* in February, 1877 and December of that year his life had reached a critical point.

Other known facts of later time speak of his somewhat different attitude to the ballet. For instance, he was obviously concerned about its future. This is confirmed, albeit indirectly, by Laroche's review published in Golos (Herald) magazine on 10 September, 1878. In that article Laroche strongly insists on producing *Swan Lake* in St. Petersburg. "*Swan Lake* must be staged... in St. Petersburg," he writes, hinting at the same time at a possible amendment and revision of the original version. "It would be unfair not to let St. Petersburg audiences hear the marvelous work of such a great master as Tchaikovsky," the critic repeats, and he returns to this subject in conclusion: "I want to make it clear that the composer's name alone is sufficient for *Swan Lake* to appear on our best stage."

Musicologists tend to ignore Laroche's vigorous arguments in favor of staging Tchaikovsky's ballet in St. Petersburg. It is obvious, however, that Laroche, who was close to the composer, expressed not only his own opinion. Tchaikovsky was evidently hurt by the indifference of the St. Petersburg ballet to *Swan Lake*. In practical terms this foreboded oblivion of its music, because only new productions could prolong its life.

The Moscow production still enjoyed moderate success but it was clear that it would not survive in the repertory longer than other ballets. Moreover, the Bolshoi choreographers allowed themselves too much leeway in handling the music of *Swan Lake*, taking advantage of the composer's absence from Moscow, so that "nearly a full third" of the score was replaced with "inserts from other ballets," as evidenced by the music critic Nikolai Kashkin, and that was a portent of death.

Swan Lake might very well be dropped from the repertoire in any season, so the further destiny of its music seemed very uncertain at the time. Kashkin writes that the composer hoped that "some numbers in the ballet will become popular as ball dances, but this hope did not come true..." This evidence is very interesting, although we do not know when Tchaikovsky said that. We can see that he was not indifferent to the fate of his music, although he expected what seems to us a strange future for it.

We can regard the composer's desire, a rather unexpected one, to remake *Swan Lake* into a suite as another attempt to save its music. Significantly, he expressed it in a letter to the music publisher Peter Jurgensson dated 20 September, 1882. At that time *Swan Lake* was not in the Bolshoi repertoire, and although it was a temporary interval, it lasted for a good two years. Tchaikovsky writes of his "desire to preserve from oblivion...music which contains a few decent pieces." He complains in the letter about the precarious existence of ballets. Indeed, in the next two years — 1882 and 1883 — *Swan Lake* was performed on stage only four times, after which it vanished from the playbills of the Russian ballet theater for twelve years.

Of course, we would not venture to say that Tchaikovsky loved his music of *Swan Lake*. It is indisputable, however, that he followed with interest the events in the stage life of his firstborn in the genre of ballet and never considered his experiment in this art a total failure. It was not accidental, therefore, that shortly before he died, Tchaikovsky had again turned to *Swan Lake* and entered into negotiations with the Directorate of the Imperial Theaters for its production in St. Petersburg.

Tchaikovsky's Reform

Tchaikovsky's first attempt to compose a ballet can be traced back to a time before *Swan Lake*, an argument often invoked by musicologists to prove that he followed a definite system of aesthetic principles in his work on the latter.

Indeed, in 1870 Tchaikovsky set out to compose the ballet *Sandrillona* to be staged at the Bolshoi, but he shortly abandoned it for unknown reasons. Some of his biographers conjecture that he was discouraged from further efforts by his revulsion for intrigues in the midst of the theatrical community.

However credible this story may be, that episode can be related to *Swan Lake* as much as all other works he created in Moscow can be qualified as its precursors.

His bold decision to compose a ballet was not a digression from principles discordant with the nature of his talent and outlook on life. He remained faithful to his romantic creed in developing his favorite themes and in applying to the genre of ballet the aesthetic principles he had embraced in symphony and opera.

So he did not follow a deliberate plan of radical revisions in the genre of dance music but naturally continued the key trends in his music of the 1860s and 1870s.

"...I am at a loss to see why the concept of ballet music should imply something reprehensible," he wrote in a letter to Taneyev.

They had an argument about Tchaikovsky's *Fourth Symphony*. For all his high opinion of it, Taneyev objected to what he described as "something like ballet music audible in each of its movements."

That was a matter of principle to Tchaikovsky. Julia Rozanova, a notable researcher on Tchaikovsky's ballet music, writes that "the composer believed that dance motifs do not detract from the quality of music but make it more dynamic."

Tchaikovsky used dance motifs in his *First* and *Second Symphonies*. The *Third Symphony* he had composed shortly before *Swan Lake* is pervaded with dance motifs of a strikingly theatrical fairy tale character. The dance rhythms and melodies were suggested by the cultural atmosphere of Moscow's social life. Waltzes and polonaises were indispensable attributes of the endless balls and masquerades Tchaikovsky often attended during his Moscow period.

At that distant time a ball was an event veiled in a romantic aura and full of promise of romantic meetings. We can visualize Tchaikovsky as a romantic hero feeling lonely and bored to death at a Moscow masquerade. At times, however, he did not mind taking part in a merry trick, such as making a bet with his friend Kashkin whereby each of them was to make up his face and wear a costume that would not let anybody recognize them at a masquerade.

The musicologist Boris Asafiev writes that Tchaikovsky was literally enchanted by the magic of the waltz, which was the most popular dance at the time. The composer viewed waltz motifs as a means of making serious music democratic, more comprehensible to the common people. Dance motifs provided a link with real life. In *Swan Lake* waltzes account for a significant part of the score.

As Julia Rozanova writes, "*Swan Lake*, Tchaikovsky's first ballet, had been prepared by a long period of creative works." That was composing dance scenes in operas and piano pieces in various dance forms, and, finally, symphonies in which a dance motif often keynoted individual movements. These experiments were the sources of Tchaikovsky's reform in the field of ballet music.

Tchaikovsky's reply to Taneyev in a letter two years after completing the ballet was in fact a statement of principles in which he expressed his distinctive aesthetic creed. He resolutely rejected any hierarchy in musical genres and pointed out the possibility of their mutual enrichment by a symphonic method common to any kind of music.

He followed this aesthetic principle in *Swan Lake* in which he outlined for the first time the way of symphonic transformation, not simply of dance music but ballet music intended for the stage. The symphonic method widened its possibilities. The music now was not the rhythmic pattern of the choreography but conveyed an artistic message of its own.

The Destiny of Swan Lake

Admiring *Sylvia* compared with which, as we know, *Swan Lake* seemed "pure crap" to Tchaikovsky, he described the finest merit of Delibes' ballet in this phrase: "This is the first ballet in which the music constitutes the best and only interest to the listener."

It is not his overestimation of Delibes' music that matters. Another thing is more important: Tchaikovsky ignored not only its embodiment in dance but also the very primitive dramaturgy. He evidently believed that the wonderful qualities of Delibes' music would make it a lasting success in contrast to *Swan Lake*, whose music dissatisfied him.

For all its wonderful qualities, however, Delibes' music failed to compensate for the weaknesses of the dramaturgical development of the ballet, so *Sylvia*, alas, did not outlast its time.

Swan Lake by contrast was destined to live a long and rich stage life and win worldwide popularity no other ballet can claim with the sole exception, perhaps, of *Giselle*.

Tchaikovsky had not, of course, foreseen this happy change in the destiny of *Swan Lake*, and small wonder! He regarded his work as a matter of course without thinking much of what eventually would give it a life of eternity. The mystery of this success lies not only in the beauty of his music but also in its profound poetic message and romantic inspiration, the psychological conflict in the characters of the heroes whose destinies so unusual and eventful, hold the attention of any audience.

Needless to say, Tchaikovsky certainly knew better which of his works deserved more acclaim. So we have to accept his judgment of *Swan Lake* as not the top of the best as far as its music is concerned. He was certainly right in his superlative description of *The Sleeping Beauty* as a ballet symphony. Neither *The Sleeping Beauty* nor *The Nutcracker*, however, can vie with *Swan Lake* for success or fame.

We shall be pleased to listen to the music of *The Sleeping Beauty* at a concert, for instance. But we will certainly want to see *Swan Lake* on stage with our own eyes, though none of the stage versions of this ballet can compare with *The Sleeping Beauty* choreographed by Petipa.

We shall listen to the music of *The Sleeping Beauty* as a wonderful composition without paying much heed to the dance. *Swan Lake*, however, is a story ballet with real-life emotions and passions where nothing is abstract or philosophically vague.

The tradition of *Swan Lake* dates from the romantic era of *La Sylphide* and *Giselle*, in which drama is the keynote of the action and the destinies of the characters. Tchaikovsky evidently did not think much of the "dramatic" merits of *Swan Lake* but assessed it as a composer. This holds true of Delibes' *Sylvia* as well.

Tchaikovsky's one-sided approach to the art of ballet and his own music is easy to explain. "Practice" contradicted "theory" here, since *Swan Lake* revealed a perfectly new interpretation of the ballet genre.

In Tchaikovsky's time the ballet theater did not demand much of the composer, obliging him to concentrate on the rhythm and metrical structure of musical numbers. The composer was to invent music for dance scenes woven into a "plot" of short episodes of pantomime and symbolic narrative, all these following a plan prepared in advance.

Tchaikovsky composed *Swan Lake* under an identical scheme. It was accidental, therefore, that once he had gotten an order for *Swan Lake* his first enquiries were about the measure and duration of dance numbers required for the ballet. That was the first and main demand made on a ballet composer which Tchaikovsky tried to meet as best he could.

In fact, the 19th-century ballet theater had no need for a dramatist composer and relied on its own time-honored laws of the action, on the rules and methods derived from its practical experience. The composer was granted a measure of leeway in the dramaturgy of the score. In other words, he could handle this problem the way he thought best. Or else he could ignore it at will without fearing reproach.

The unity of music and dance, or — to be more accurate — music, dance and drama, had not yet become an all-important problem and remained, as a rule, outside the ballet theater's field of vision.

A ballet performance was, in effect, just another form of the ordinary dance concert, though in disguise. The St. Petersburg ballet as a cultural phenomenon in its own right was actually an integral part of royal court entertainment. Divertissement,

Tchaikovsky in repose: 1893.

for which the Russian classical ballet has been censured, was its guiding aesthetic and ideological principle. The plot was also a mask. It was just play meant to humor a sophisticated high society audience least of all interested to see lifelike action on the stage.

Even a tragedy was presented as a magnificent theatrical spectacle at that theater of masquerade. One can only wonder what excited the audience more: the death of the heroes drowned by the waves of the stormy lake or the miraculous sight of the raging elements presented on the stage with great skill and imagination.

Incidentally, the critic Kashkin was indignant when he heard the thunderous noise on the stage in the finale of *Swan Lake*. "The rumble of the powerful stage machinery drowned the music altogether," he wrote in a review. One may be amused to learn that his rebuke should have been addressed to Tchaikovsky, because it was on the latter's initiative that Waltz arranged a "veritable deluge" on the stage.

Tchaikovsky believed in the primacy of music in ballet and sought to free it from its slavery to the tradition of theatrical splendor. In his view, the ideal ballet is one whose music could be enjoyed as much as any good instrumental composition without relevance to the conventions of the ballet stage.

That was evidently the aim Tchaikovsky pursued in composing *Swan Lake* and the reason why he deemed its dramatic side a matter of secondary importance.

A Quest of Ideal Love

This is an excerpt from Tchaikovsky's letter to his father:

"Dear Papa:

"Your son Pyotr has made up his mind to have a family. Since he hates the idea of wedlock without his father's consent, he is asking you to give your blessing to his matrimony.

"I am going to marry the maiden Antonina Ivanovna Milyukova. She is a poor but very good and honest girl, and she loves me very much.

"Dad, you know that one of my age would not venture to get married until after sober consideration, so you need not worry about me. I am sure that my future wife will do her best to make my life quiet and happy."

A quest of "quiet" and "happiness" is the key motif of almost all music composed by Tchaikovsky in Moscow. This is a quest of ideal feminine beauty and ideal exalted love.

34

Swan Lake is the culmination of this theme, which first appeared in vague outline in *Ondine*, his second opera which he destroyed, as well as in other compositions of his Moscow period: the symphonic fantasias *Romeo and Juliet*, *The Storm*, *Francesca da Rimini*, and the music for the fairy tale, *The Snow Maiden*.

Ondine, *Julia*, *Francesca*, *Miranda*, *The Snow Maiden* and, finally, *Odette*, the heroine of *Swan Lake*, all belonged to a world of real and fantastic women where unfaithfulness and hypocrisy were unthinkable. They would be joined by *Tatiana* from the opera *Eugene Onegin*, Tchaikovsky's last heroine of the Moscow period, who embodies what he regarded as the supreme endowment of a woman, that of lofty and passionate self-sacrifice.

Tchaikovsky saw an illusion of that endowment in his fiancée. Like Pushkin's *Tatiana*, she wrote a love letter which surprised and moved the composer. That letter sealed her fate and opened a Pandora's box of her misfortunes. Kashkin claimed that Tchaikovsky heard in his love story an echo of *Eugene Onegin*, which occupied his mind at the time.

However, his attempt to construct in real life a model of absolute supreme happiness ended in a disaster. The magic of artistic imagination had proved helpless against the prosaic side of life. A romantic dream ended in a cruel real-life situation where hatred and enmity left no room for lyrical emotions.

Explaining the motives for his marriage in a letter to Mme von Meck, Tchaikovsky writes of the fatal force of circumstances, the sign of destiny that cannot be escaped and his fatal attraction to "this girl." For Milyukova too, her love for Tchaikovsky, — and she loved him with all the passion and sincerity of youth, — was also an almost fatal compulsion that drove her to violent despair.

She had a vague ideal of her true part in that story and instinctively protested against her dubitable position. Tchaikovsky idealized her, a poor thing hopelessly in love, but she resisted (and that was her tragic mistake) any idealization and was unwilling to be a guardian angel bringing peace and tranquility to the tormented soul of an artist "tired of living."

Tchaikovsky's music failed to capture her imagination and it was not for his talent that she loved him. She was not familiar with his compositions; this was incomprehensible to him. Indeed, he could not understand why a woman who loved him dearly should be almost indifferent to his music. As a composer and artist he could not resign himself to this fact, which lent a special inner meaning to his disillusionment with his wife.

The role of *Ondine*, *Julia* or *Tatiana* was just as detestable to Milyukova as the role of a respectable Moscow bourgeois, the head of a family enjoying the sensual pleasure of peaceful marital love was to Tchaikovsky. This "paradise" in which the dream of ideal love came true in a grotesque and twisted form was a quagmire where he would choke to death.

Who knows, but this story of Tchaikovsky's marriage may be overly romantic. But let us recall what one of his closest friends, the critic Kashkin, wrote.

"One must be thoroughly familiar with Tchaikovsky's nature to understand the intimate relationship between his own life and the life of the heroes of his compositions."

In Kashkin's view that was crucial to a faithful and accurate interpretation of all the events of Tchaikovsky's marriage. He was an artist who "worshipped the ideal woman as an equal partner and even the guardian angel of a man." Kashkin writes further that Tchaikovsky's marriage "was a critical event in his life his future biographers should analyze in detail to understand his moral principles and his outlook on life and man."

The young Tchaikovsky had a romantic view of the world in which art and life are mingled and the artist's life is governed by a special "literary" logic of development. His own life becomes a theme of art and assumes unexpected, fanciful romantic features. Romanticism created its own poetry and method and its own type of the artist's biography.

Tchaikovsky continued the traditions of European romanticism which had formed the image of an ideal beloved, an *Ondine* with a selfless and chaste soul opposed to the cruelty of the world and the prosaic reality of life. *Swan Lake* was probably the last composition in this romantic vein in all European culture.

Laroche who had read *Ondine* in his declining years was charmed by the "naive fairy tale romance of the poem" and amazed by the "profound affinity of the poetry of that period and Tchaikovsky's cast of mind and emotional make-up." He writes in his reminiscences of Tchaikovsky that the latter "was under the influence...of the French poets of the 1830s, particularly Alfred de Musset, whom he admired. It was from these Frenchmen that he had borrowed the graceful carelessness so often audible in his music." As evidenced by Laroche, Tchaikovsky in the 1870s and 1880s impressed one as a romantic who had "preserved...the tastes of the times of Louis Philippe."

In the period from *Ondine* composed by Tchaikovsky in 1869 to *Swan Lake* seven years later, romantic art seemed to relive its history in an instant revival of its beauty and power. The image of *Odette,* the heroine of *Swan Lake,* an ideal incarnation of heavenly love tragically unattainable, was also in a way the last of such female images created by Tchaikovsky.

Concerning One Delusion

A number of editions devoted to *Swan Lake*, in particular the book of C.W. Beaumont published in London in 1952, claim as a fact that Tchaikovsky had improvised the images of his future ballet long before 1875 when he started composing it. In 1871 he had allegedly composed a one-act ballet of the same name for A.I. Davydova's children, in the village of Kamenka.

Some information on a short children's ballet called *The Lake of Swans* is to be found in the reminiscences of Y.L. Davydov and A.L. Davydova-Meck, Tchaikovsky's nephew and niece respectively. On the basis of this evidence, a story of the ballet composed at Kamenka was included in the chronicle of Tchaikovsky's life and work published in 1940 under the title *P.I. Tchaikovsky's Days and Years*.

The evidence of Y.L. and A.L. Davydov, however, can hardly be taken at its face value. For instance, Anna Lvovna Davydova-Meck related the ballet staged at Kamenka to the year 1867 when she was only three years of age. For his part, Yuri Lvovich Davydov mentioned the year 1871, referring to what he had learned from the older members of his family; he was born in 1876. In fact, A.L. Davydova-Meck recalled that children's ballet in very old age, more than seventy years later.

There is another strange fact: the composer's biography, written by his brother Modest Tchaikovsky, makes no mention of the ballet staged at Kamenka, although, as is evidenced by A.L. Davydova-Meck, he had played the part of the Prince in it, and so he was supposed to know about the ballet.

Of course, some ballet with a name like *Swan Lake* was staged at Kamenka, but when that event took place and whether it had any relation to the ballet we know is a matter for guesses. A.L. Davydova-Meck admitted that she did not remember the music of that ballet for children. Nor did she remember the plot, recalling only that wooden swans had long been kept in their home after the performance and that she had played the part of Cupid in it.

Y.L. Davydova, on the contrary, said confidently that "the main theme — the song of swans — was the same as in the music we know and that in his later large composition Tchaikovsky had used the themes of the children's ballet of 1871."

We cannot take this evidence at its face value, of course. However, it sheds light on some events connected with the origin of the score of *Swan Lake*, since none of its drafts has been found to date.

Tchaikovsky did not compose the music specially for the children's ballet. He had most likely used his earlier compositions he might have later included in *Swan Lake*, naturally after considerable revisions.

What kind of music could that be? We can only make conjectures on this subject. Take, for instance, the missing sketches of *Sandrillona*, if the ballet was really staged at Kamenka in 1871, or fragments from *Ondine*. Who knows, was it not the latter that suggested the "swan theme" so close in intonation and melody to the adagio of Siegfried and Odette taken by Tchaikovsky from the opera he had destroyed?

The children's ballet staged at Kamenka confirms an important circumstance in the history of composing *Swan Lake*: Tchaikovsky had evidently compiled the score of this ballet of pieces of his earlier music, adapting it to the requirements of another genre. It is definitely known that Tchaikovsky had borrowed the prelude to the fourth act of *Swan Lake* from the prelude to the third act of the opera *Voivode*. The scene and dance of little swans are also based on the themes of this opera, and one can easily discern an echo of the overture to the composer's first opera in the introduction to *Swan Lake*. One may add to this the aforementioned adagio of Siegfried and Odette which was transferred to *Swan Lake* from *Ondine*.

As for the music of *Voivode*, restored from orchestral parts since the score of that opera was destroyed by Tchaikovsky, today we have a fairly good idea of it.

But what about the sketches of *Sandrillona* and the multi-act score of *Ondine* with which none of the composer's friends was acquainted? That is a significant fact in itself. It is not unlikely that the inserts of music Tchaikovsky had composed earlier into the score of *Swan Lake* were not isolated.

This may be explained by the severe time shortage the composer was plagued by in composing the ballet and the distinctive character of his attitude to his work: Tchaikovsky invariably tried to preserve whatever music he had composed. As evidenced by Kashkin, he requested a fantastic or chivalrous subject, accepting an order for composing the ballet. He was probably trying to select a subject adaptable to available musical material in themes and ideas.

Coming back to the children's ballet at Kamenka, we should note that the most mysterious thing about it is not the music but the plot. Presuming that it was close in subject to *Swan Lake*, we should conclude that Tchaikovsky himself initiated the choice of the theme of *Swan Lake* and that it was a long known fairy tale with which he was familiar.

This conjecture, however, is disproved by Tchaikovsky's letter to Laroche: "According to a story by Jurgensson, the libretto of *Swan Lake* was invented by Begichev, but the copy available to the Directorate of the Imperial Theaters bears a hand-written inscription which says: *Geltzer's* library. The latter had probably recounted it in writing. The stupid plot and the names of the characters show that the libretto was made by one of these two persons."

An artist's conception of Tchaikovsky.

It is clear from Tchaikovsky's letter that the plot of *Swan Lake* had not been known to him before and that any home-made fairy tale is out of the question here. So the children's ballet at Kamenka with its Cupid and wooden swans had, of course, no relation to the composer's future ballet.

Tchaikovsky started his work on *Swan Lake* in May 1875 and ended it at Glebovo on April 10, 1876. That was the date he marked on the final manuscript of the score: "The End! Glebovo. April 10, 1876."

In the meantime individual numbers of the first act were already being rehearsed at the Bolshoi. On February 20, 1877 Moscow's audience heard Tchaikovsky's new composition: his first ballet, *Swan Lake*. That was the first night of this masterpiece of Russian and world classical art.

The Origin of the Plot

The fairy tale *Swan Pond* by the Austrian author Museus was first mentioned as a probable literary source of *Swan Lake*, by Y.I. Slonimsky, an eminent student of Tchaikovsky's ballets. True, the fairy tale appeared in Russian translation some time after the ballet had been composed. The fairy tale, however, might have been known from German or French editions. It is not unlikely that Reisinger, for whom Museus was almost a fellow countryman, had played a part in selecting this fairy tale.

Indeed, in Museus's tale there are a number of details which were possibly borrowed by the librettists of *Swan Lake*. Slonimsky describes some of these details: "The scenario writers of the ballet could have taken the name (the authentic title of Museus's fairy tale is "Stolen Veils". The revision of the title in the Russian translation is very significant) and the scene at the lake where swans flock together and turn into beautiful princesses at night. In the ballet, the Prince's friend, the chevalier Benno, has the same name as in the fairy tale. Just as in the ballet an evil knight, though possessing no magic powers, stands in the way of the heroes aspiring towards happiness."

All these arguments are conclusive, of course, but what matters most is this: Tchaikovsky's *Swan Lake* is close to Museus's fairy tale in his interpretation of the image of the swan princess. The original scenario for which the music was composed has been practically forgotten today. In the original scenario, for instance, there is no evil magician Rothbart, no struggle between him and Siegfried in the finale, and no enchanted swan maidens languishing in their dreadful captivity.

We are familiar with a different *Swan Lake* and a different scenario written for the St. Petersburg production of 1895, after Tchaikovsky's death. Whereas in all productions of *Swan Lake* we know Odette and her friends are maidens under the spell of Rothbart's magic, in the libretto of 1877 Odette was not an ordinary human maiden forcibly turned into a swan.

The librettists and the composer called Odette a good fairy. She is a magic and mysterious being governing the forces of nature protecting her against human perfidy and malicious witchcraft.

In the production of Petipa and Ivanov, Odette has a natural desire to become a human maiden. She wants to get rid of the magic spell and discard her swan wings which are an obstacle to her happy and lawful marriage. Her love for Siegfried is happiness and her life on the lake is captivity; deliverance from this imprisonment is the purpose of her struggle and the message of the ballet, whose events in their present form develop the idea of salvation from evil magic.

Tchaikovsky's Odette is a different being. Her life on the lake is the natural life of a fairy, and she takes it for granted. She is like one of the swan maidens in Museus's fairy-tale. There are no bewitched princesses here but there are fairies in the image of swans, which is a symbol of eternal life and youth. In Tchaikovsky's ballet, Odette and her maiden friends could turn into swans at will, because they were magic beings by nature.

In Museus' fairy tale the swan maidens differ from ordinary swans by wearing a crown of feathers. In all productions we know the swans of the corps de ballet and Odette herself wear such crowns. Today, however, this ornamental detail has a different meaning: it is a symbol of swan life. This is a magic crown. The hero who steals the crown deprives the fairy of her magic powers. Without her crown she is no longer a fairy but an ordinary human maiden. This can make her happy, but now she is exposed to danger like any human being. When she lives as a fairy, however, no human ills or evil forces can threaten her.

The motif of the "crown" was decisive in the *Swan Lake* composed by Tchaikovsky. Her crown protected Odette from the crafty designs of her vicious step-mother who lived in an ancient tower on the lake shore. In the finale of the ballet Siegfried took the crown off the head of Odette, trying to force her to stay with him against her will, because she could not forgive the Prince's unfaithfulness at the ball and wanted to escape from the lake.

That action of Siegfried was the cause of their death. Odette's step-mother in the image of an owl flew over the lake, squeaking ominously and carrying the crown thrown off by the Prince in her claws.

As it can be inferred from the scenario, that was when Odette died, although in the production of 1877, as we can see in a drawing of the final scene of the ballet and read in reviews, Odette did not die instantly but she and Siegfried "were fighting for their lives, holding on to a tree branch amidst the raging waves."

The owl step-mother was guilty of her death indirectly, and Odette said to Siegfried that he alone was to blame for their death. The evil fate in the image of an owl took advantage of the human error committed by Prince Siegfried.

The owl step-mother is the image of destiny lying in wait for man so as to punish him for any weakness or mistake, just as the image of the Mouse King in Hoffmann's *The Nutcracker*.

In later productions of the ballet after 1877 the image of the owl step-mother was deleted and replaced with Rothbart, who was a secondary character in the original conception. It is easy to explain the reasons for this revision. The authors of the libretto of 1895 sought to make the action as logical as possible and hence they objected to the two evil characters in the ballet acting separately without any visible connection between them.

However, it was impossible to expunge Rothbart, simply a demon of middle rank in Tchaikovsky's version, since he escorted Odile to the ball. Moreover, the sight of a dummy owl flying above the stage seemed ridiculous to the choreographers. As a result, the functions of the owl were handed over to Rothbart, who thus concentrated all evil of the world in his hands.

In the St. Petersburg production of 1895, therefore, Rothbart was a powerful evil magician who held the swan maidens in captivity by his witchcraft.

The revision of the main motif of the plot and the entry of Rothbart as a concrete incarnation of evil possibly made the action more logical and, what was most important, easier to comprehend than the scenario of 1877. This revision drastically simplified it. It is easy to see that the fantastic theme in the original libretto of *Swan Lake* provided the motivation for a psychological drama involving a relationship between an earthly man of flesh and blood, and a magic fairy. That was a relationship between two different worlds: the real world of human beings, and the world of fairy tale nature and poetry.

Tchaikovsky asserted the lofty and noble idea that happiness cannot be gained through violence. The culmination of the theme was the wonderful musical scene of the storm in the finale. It was the vengeance of Nature inflicted upon human being for destruction of heavenly harmony and his violation of ideal beauty symbolized by Odette. That was a great chastising tempest in which Siegfried met his death atoning for the evil he had brought to the world of poetry and harmony.

The ancient fairy tale of *Ondine* was crucial to developing the image of Odette, and the theme of the ballet as a whole, as it was in Tchaikovsky's conception. *Ondine* is a water sprite in folklore, but Odette, too, is a water fairy in the first place and a "swan" in the second.

Just as Ondine, she meets a knight, an earthly human being, and learns of his unfaithfulness. Many motifs from *Ondine* are present in *Swan Lake*, and the swan theme is also partly a borrowing from *Ondine*.

After Ondine's death the chevalier Hulbrandt has a strange dream of mystical significance, in which he makes a mysterious journey on swan wings ("as though he was lifted by these wings into the air, and he flew above the earth and waters with a gentle and sweet-voiced wind.")

The swan image has no concrete meaning here. The swans are the messengers of Ondine, an image metaphor of imminent death: "A swan song! A swan song!... It is a herald of death."

At a birthday festival, at a time of joy and merriment, Siegfried sees a flock of swans flying above the park. A foreboding of disaster disturbs the world of carefree enjoyment of life and fills his heart with anguish and fear. The swan image allures him as the supreme embodiment of beauty, but the appearance of a flock of swans above the luxuriant palace park in the very beginning of the act portends death. Siegfried runs to the lake and meets his doom.

Using a duet from the opera *Ondine* he had destroyed for the music of the adagio of Odette and Siegfried, Tchaikovsky pursued not only practical aims. This duet contrasts in character with the dances surrounding it in the ballet.

The duet is full of sorrow with audible intonations of weeping and plaintive supplication somewhat unexpectedly disturbing the serene and happy scene of swan play with its jubilant waltz, the mischievous scherzo of swans (to whose music Ivanov would later stage the famous dance of little swans), the graceful and slightly capricious solo of Odette, and the dynamic, swift and bravura coda concluding it all.

In the adagio of Odette and Siegfried there is no joy of a first declaration of love, which was required by the librettists. An adagio of this character could have been more proper in the finale of the ballet as a duet of farewell and parting. The inevitable anticipation of it is the meaning of the duet culminating the second act.

The adagio of Odette and Siegfried is based on the motifs of the duet of Ondine and Hulbrandt. Odette is not worried about her bitter fate as a swan, but she is aggrieved by the destiny of Siegfried who is doomed to death and regrets her fatal meeting that is bound to bring disaster to them.

Ondine also implored Hulbrandt to be faithful to her not only because she loved him. She feared for his life, because she knew that if he should prove unfaithful to her, he would seal his own fate and pass a death verdict on himself. She desired passionately to save him from sure death but could do nothing to ward it off. She mourned his death, anticipating his inevitable unfaithfulness.

Tchaikovsky himself showed us the closeness of *Swan Lake* to *Ondine* by taking from this opera a duet for one of the finest and most poetic episodes of the ballet. It was, perhaps, on account of this duet that he regarded the second act of *Swan Lake* as the best of all others. Recalling his early opera *Ondine* shortly before his death, Tchaikovsky wrote that "some of its music seems to be very sincere and good."

Although the composer never regretted his destruction of *Ondine*, he evidently had a special affection for its music as long as he lived.

A definite relationship between the initial scenario of *Swan Lake* and *Ondine* is audible in a number of episodes the ballet and the fairy tale have in common. It is obvious, for instance, that the episode in which Hulbrandt takes the necklace off Ondine's neck, after which she dies, is indirectly reflected in the scene of Siegfried taking the crown off Odette's head in the finale of the ballet. The scene of the storm must have been borrowed from *Ondine* also. The meaning of this scene is, in effect, identical in the tale and in the ballet.

The Moscow Première

We know little about the first production of *Swan Lake* in 1877. Reviewers were unanimous in their negative appraisals of it but left practically no description of its details. Our judgment on the general conception and individual episodes of the ballet, therefore, is based on a detailed playbill of the première that has survived to date.

Playbills of that time differed significantly from what they are today. They invariably listed all numbers and all dances in each act. A careful analysis provides interesting material for reflection and discussion.

We know, for instance, from the playbill of the première of *Swan Lake*, that a new character absent in the libretto existed in the first action of Reisinger's production.

Poselanka (Peasant Maiden) took part in four of the seven numbers of the first act. She was danced by Maria Stanislavskaya. She was presented on the playbill in three episodes as a partner of Guillerd-II who danced Siegfried. Though nameless, this character obviously played a significant part in the action linked to the theme of beautiful and carefree youth, the theme of Siegfried's last love affair before a new page opened in his life.

Just as in Tchaikovsky's score the action of the ballet opened with a waltz in which four peasant maidens danced solo parts. Stanislavskaya was one of them.

The dance scene, and the coming of the governing Princess who announced Siegfried's forthcoming marriage, was followed by the pas de deux of Siegfried and Poselanka (Peasant Maiden). Today this pas de deux is missing from the first act of the ballet.

Ricardo Drigo, conductor of the St. Petersburg production of *Swan Lake*, and Marius Petipa, who had "composed" their own ballet on the basis of Tchaikovsky's music, transferred the duet to the third act, where it was to be danced by Siegfried and Odile.

In Reisinger's production, however, the pas de deux had its place in the first act. In the scenario, after Siegfried's mother had left, the chevalier Benno comforted Siegfried and urged him to continue the merrymaking and enjoy life while it was still possible. The author's remarks in the score evidence that this denouement of the episode was preserved by Tchaikovsky and the choreographers. The festive, open-hearted and cheerful duet of Siegfried and Poselanka was a response to Benno's appeal.

In the first act of Reisinger's production, Siegfried evidently played an active part in the various episodes, not only by pantomime but also by dance. The scattered episodes were grouped, as it were, around the main hero advanced to the foreground, creating an integral composition of stage action.

Every episode helped reveal Siegfried's character, reflecting his emotions, moods, and thoughts. That was a very important component of the Moscow production of 1877, which had not been duly comprehended until Yuri Grigorovich's production. That was probably the reason why the first scene of the ballet had long been a stumbling block even for the most talented choreographers.

Yuri Grigorovich made this comment:

"As I see it, we have always taken a superficial view of the version of 1877, arguing that it was a 'failure' according to the consensus of opinion. It will be recalled, however, that Tchaikovsky himself was involved in that 'failure'.

"The production was prepared in his lifetime, and he attended rehearsals, as we know, had discussions with the choreographer, gave him advice and added some finishing touches to the score, with members of the cast in a work-out on individual scenes as he watched them.

"All that should be remembered, particularly when it comes to the most sophisticated acts of the ballet — the first and the third — where a sequence of numbers, unconnected by the outward logic of dramaturgy, has often led choreographers to the convention of ordinary divertissement veiled with situational details.

"The main question, however, is how is one to interpret, for instance, this first scene in the general context of the events in the ballet? As a prologue, a prelude to the central swan scene? Or as a definite stage of the drama, not informational but crucial to further events?

"Petipa considered the first scene in isolation from the other acts of the ballet as merely a topical motivation for developing the action. Indeed, there was a festival with dances which could be varied in number regardless of the subject and meaning of the action. And there was an event of the plot: a file of swans flying above the park.

Odette, as portrayed by Marina Semyonova.

"It was from this point that the ballet actually began. The preceding events had roughly outlined the hero's portrait as a young and cheerful man. That was all there was in Siegfried's characterization.

"In Tchaikovsky's music, however, the first act is the clue to understanding the drama that will happen much later."

Grigorovich is certainly right. Though Siegfried has practically no musical theme of his own in the score, he is precisely the main personage in the first act, which may be regarded as a peculiar inner monologue of the hero.

All the music of the first act is the music of Siegfried, just as all the music of the second act is the music of Odette. This is how these two acts might have been called in the ballet.

In this sense the third act seems to have blended these two musical worlds into a common whole. It will be recalled, however, that at Siegfried's ball Odette could appear only in the image of Odile. A transition from one world to another demands an "external" transformation as well. Another thing is more important: Odile brings to Siegfried's ball the themes and intonations of "swan music," her doubts, torments and fatal charms.

This music seems to tear apart the fabric of decorous divertissement peculiar to a court festival. It plays havoc with the habitual "order" and brings "chaos" into a life of tranquility. In the pas de deux, expunged in Petipa's production, this blending of two different musical worlds has a dramatic denouement: a "swan song", a lament, disrupts the steady pattern of the charming dances of the brides.

The fourth act is a return to the world of Odette, the final resolution of the drama, the relentless steps of destiny and the heroes' death in the violent storm on the lake. The theme of the lake surrounding the "swan acts" of the ballet literally floods everything and reaches an unusually powerful culmination in the finale.

Odette is the main heroine of the ballet. The image of Siegfried, however, determines its action. He comes to the lake shore, where he meets Odette and falls in love with her. Then he returns to the castle and becomes infatuated with Odile, forgetful of his chosen swan beloved, and dooms her to death in the finale.

This is why the first scene of the ballet is the point of departure for all further events. All its fragments and numbers prepare, in effect, the "swan acts", foreshadowing the hero's rupture with the world, calling him to escape rather than go a-hunting, and create a poetic image of doubt and anxious anticipation of change in his destiny.

Odette is now in his thoughts and dreams, so the swans flying above the park mean to him the sign of destiny, not just birds good for a huntsman's trophy.

It is easy to guess that Reisinger totally failed in the second "swan" act. Reviewers unanimously praised Waltz' imaginative work here. They commented in detail on his technical innovation: the use of steam to create an illusion of fog drifting over the lake. But they said almost nothing about the dances.

It is only known that the swan corps de ballet performed some rhythmic motions, which left the audience unimpressed. As evidenced by D. Lyashkov, a known balletomane who had seen the première, "the swimming swans were depicted by the corps de ballet aligned in ranks behind long lengths of tulle stretched across the full breadth of the stage, which depicted water, with only the heads of the dancers clearly visible to the audience."

If that was really so, Reisinger's "swans" certainly looked ridiculous.

Tchaikovsky's remarks add little to the reviewers' comments. He never mentions the chevalier Benno, although the latter must have been present on the stage not only during Siegfried's meeting with Odette but also when she was telling the Prince about her life in which happiness and sadness were strangely mingled. Benno's presence in that scene must have looked incongruous, too.

Incidentally, in the Petipa-Ivanov production Benno as Siegfried's true friend was reluctant to leave him even in the most intimate episodes and helped him to perform the adagio with Odette, supporting the ballerina whenever the Prince was unable to do it himself. Pavel Herdt who danced the Prince was almost sixty at the time, so the choreographers had decided to compensate for his physical weakness by this strange method.

We know from the playbill of the Moscow première in which only choreographic numbers are listed that there were no dances in the second act before the entrance of swans. The action followed the plot in which the heroine "set out" the details of the situation. That was followed by the entrance of swans, who reproached the Prince for his cruelty, and he swore on his honor that he would never again kill a single bird. He reaffirmed his oath by breaking his gun in front of them.

Now all calmed down, and the dances began. That was how events developed in the scenario and evidently in the production, as we can see from Tchaikovsky's written remarks.

Reisinger obviously had turned the "swan" act into an habitual dance divertissement mingled with a pantomime narration of events.

The final act of the ballet in which Mr. Waltz's miracles — thunder, lightning, flood, and others — held pride of place was probably just as unsuccessful in the Moscow production.

The third act of the Moscow production, however, is of certain interest to us,

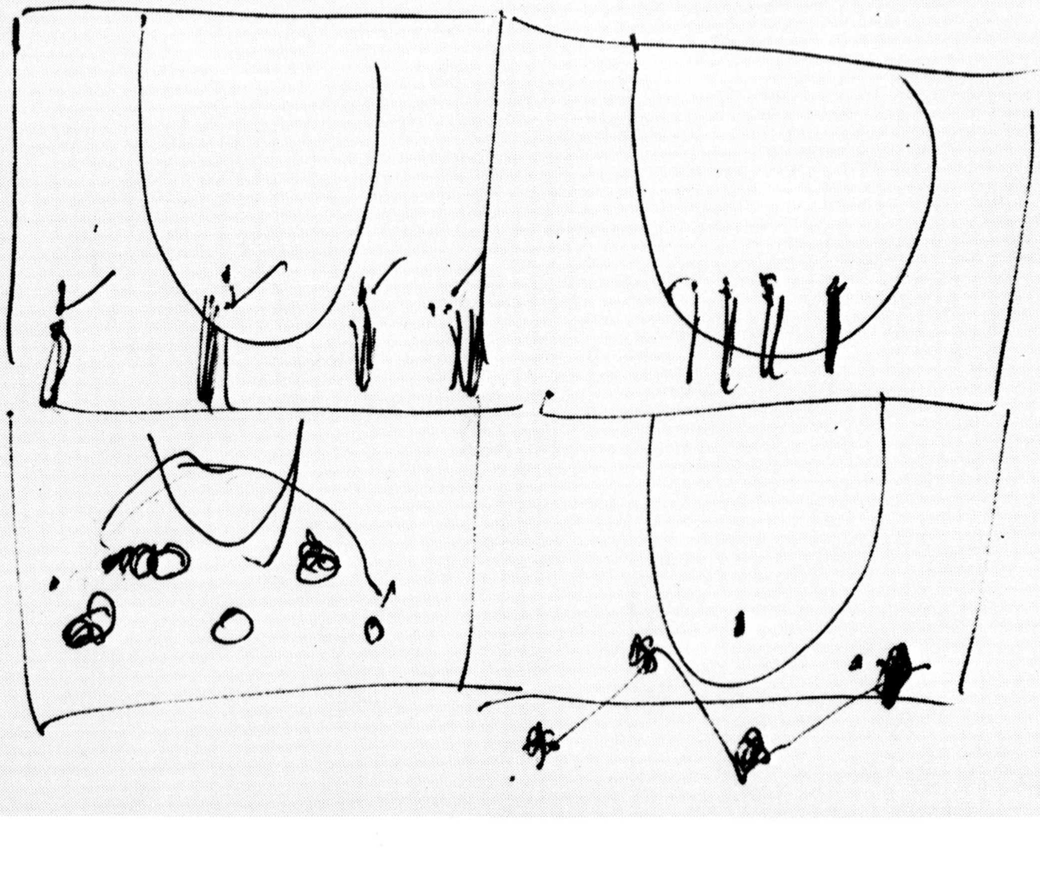

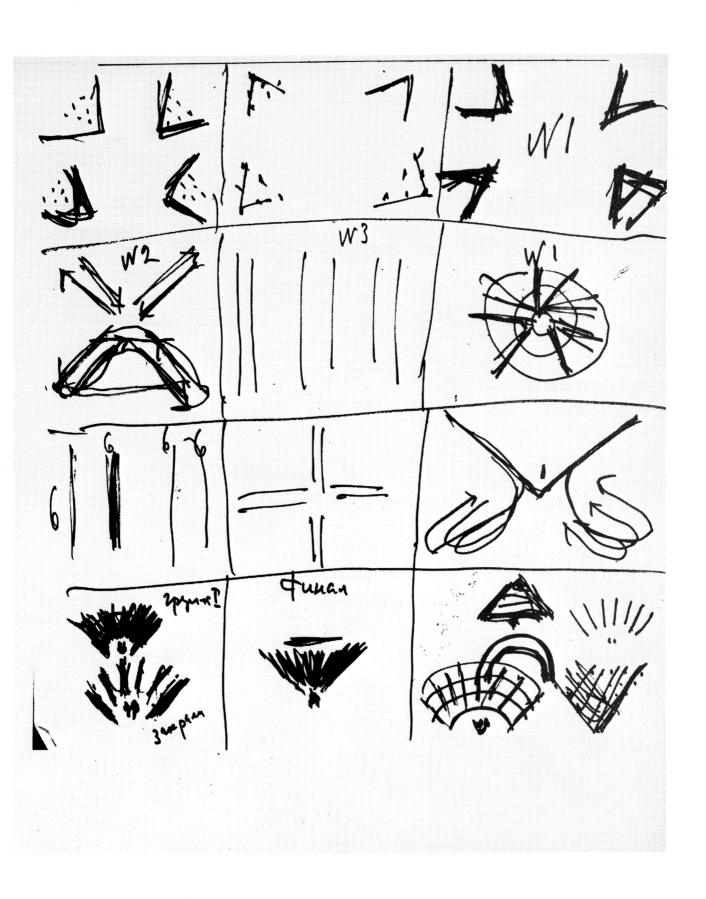

Notes and sketches by the choreographer of one of the
stagings of *Swan Lake* at the Bolshoi Ballet.

51

primarily because the music of this act was subjected to the greatest revisions and distortions in later versions of the ballet.

As it follows from the author's remarks, the action was opened by various processions and ritual preparations for a ball. That was followed by the dance of courtiers and pages listed in the playbill and the entrance of the brides. The author's remarks in this scene are slightly divergent from the libretto.

It is clear, for instance, that the four brides, as many as the Peasant Maidens (Poselankas) who had danced solo in the first act, appeared one by one, and that the entrance of each new bride was identical to the previous one.

Each girl was escorted by her parents and after dancing one turn of a waltz with a cavalier, retreated to her place among the small crowd of guests.

"After a few entrances of brides," the scenario reads, "the Princess puts to Siegfried the 'fatal question'." Then Odile came on the scene, just as in today's version.

A Fatal Likeness

The problem of the "fatal likeness" of Odette to Odile has always excited the interest of musicologists and choreographers. They assumed, not without reason, that the right answer to this problem would provide the clue to a correct interpretation of the ballet as a whole and the image of Siegfried first and foremost.

Who is Odile? A sinister and malicious imitation of Odette created by treacherous witchcraft?

Or is she Odette herself who has come to the ball to test Siegfried's loyalty?

How essential is the outward likeness between the two characters and how much alike are they?

These are logical questions, because, as we can learn from the scenario, it only seems to Siegfried that Odile looks like Odette, as is evidenced by his dialogue with Benno after the mysterious appearance of Rothbart with his daughter.

"Don't you think that she looks like Odette?" asks Siegfried. He certainly knows that he sees another maiden who reminds him of the lake fairy he met the night before. Benno immediately disagrees with him: "Not at all...you seem to see your Odette in anybody."

Indeed, Benno who had a full night of amusement along with Siegfried in the company of swan fairies sees in Odile no resemblance to Odette and even pokes fun at his infatuated friend who fancies the image of his night maiden friend everywhere. The likeness of Odile to Odette is probably not as close as we imagine. Odile only reminds him of Odette but is not her double. Moreover, she is not trying to pose as Odette.

If this is not so, why then should she call herself Odile and bring to the ball a stranger in the guise of her father?

After all, she could have come to the ball alone and called herself Odette so as to reveal at a critical moment her demoniac image the guileless Siegfried was unable to discern under her bewitching mask of love and goodness.

No, the ballet presents a different situation, and the disaster that strikes Siegfried and Odette is caused by their own human weaknesses.

Is this interpretation of the image of Siegfried too narrow? Do we not depict him as a fickle lighthearted youth who carelessly leads Odette to her doom?

Of course, if Siegfried's unfaithfulness is interpreted as an innocent act committed under the spell of witchcraft, his image appears much more favorable. But in such an event there is no drama in the ballet. One chance occurrence simply follows another without any meaning or logic. Siegfried is not guilty, nor is Odette; the only culprit is her step-mother whose intrigues cause their tragic death.

But why does Siegfried feel repentance when he comes to the lake? Why is he reproached by Odette who cannot forgive him, as said in the scenario?

No, it is not with her likeness to Odette that Odile entices Siegfried at the ball. This likeness is just one of her charms intended to tempt his virtue.

We can read in the scenario that Siegfried is amazed by Odile's beauty. It is only after some time that he realizes the likeness of her face to Odette's. He is stunned by Odile's beauty, and this is what matters most. He meets a young maiden more beautiful than Odette and looking like Odette at the same time.

This beautiful stranger lures him by her charms of artful femininity in which gracefulness and sensuality are blended to be irresistible.

Odile is an image of sensual beauty, an erotic vision which triumphs over the incorporeal image of a lake fairy with her plaintive spirit and chaste naive dreams.

Odile tempts Siegfried with a promise of carnal pleasure and her feminine sorcery, her frank emotions and pliant plastic body. Feeling Siegfried's hesitation and doubts, she provokes him by an illusion of her likeness to Odette.

Such is the meaning of the image of Odile, an evil joke of destiny, which has created this sensual phantom of sham happiness mocking the lofty idea of self-sacrificial feminine love.

A New Swan Lake

The first production of *Swan Lake* left no trace in the history of art. It is interesting, however, that in Reisinger's production Tchaikovsky's music was performed almost in full for the first and last time. He did not live to see other productions of his ballet.

In the history of the stage life of *Swan Lake* Reisinger's version holds a place of its own, because it had been a long time before the next, absolutely new, production of *Swan Lake* was staged at the Marinsky Theater of St. Petersburg as late as 1895.

Therefore, Reisinger's production can hardly be considered the starting point of the stage history of *Swan Lake*. Musicologists count its record from the production of 1895, which is fair, since it was the choreography of Petipa and Ivanov that firmly established *Swan Lake* on the ballet stage and won it broad popularity.

The version of 1895 was, in effect, a new *Swan Lake* both in subject and in music. How are we to take this fact?

Are we entitled to take an intransient stand in view of our admiration for Tchaikovsky's music and our reverential attitude to the initial conception of his ballet? Let us be reasonable and listen to the full story of *Swan Lake*. Admirers of Marius Petipa tell us that he deserves full credit for the brilliant stage life of *Swan Lake*, that without him and the contributions of Riccardo Drigo and Lev Ivanov this ballet would not have attained the pinnacles of worldwide fame today.

Alas, it is true. Indeed, in its original version *Swan Lake* would have hardly risen to its present place in the history of world art. This ballet missed its chance at birth, which, if anything, was Reisinger's historical fault.

Like *Giselle*, *Swan Lake* might have remained for us a classical chef-d'oeuvre of pure romanticism. In the late years of the 19th century, however, it was recalled from its oblivion and staged in St. Petersburg at a theater which had already produced *The Sleeping Beauty* and *The Nutcracker* and would produce Glazunov's *Raimonda* three years later.

The Marinsky Theater was already very far from the naivete of pure romanticism in its original form. Petipa had taken account of the changes that had taken place in real life and in art.

Needless to say, Petipa and Drigo's work in editing the score had caused considerable damage to it. The revision of the scenario could not be described as an improvement either. Strange as it may seem, however, all these revisions made the ballet more comprehensible and helped it gain unprecedented popularity.

The original *Swan Lake* had been burdened with too many literary details, carried a load of various time-honored traditions, and had too much psychological sophistication in spite of the outward simplicity of its dramaturgical scheme and the exquisite gracefulness of its music.

Compared with the ballet composed in 1877, the *Swan Lake* recreated by Petipa and Drigo had an important advantage: the utmost clarity and precision in developing the imagined events of a theatrical fairy tale. From a psychological novella, an "ancient legend," the ballet was transformed into a fairy tale in which good and evil are in laconic and graphic contrast to each other.

It is true, Petipa and especially Drigo went too far in some of their revisions. It was hardly necessary, to take but one example, to delete in the final act the scene of the storm, thereby depriving the musical dramaturgy of its culmination. One can only wonder, what practical purpose was pursued by the re-orchestration of the whole score? Drigo, in addition, did not have scruples about adding his own music to Tchaikovsky's composition!

There are quite a few such "absurdities" in the Petipa-Drigo version. However, it contains quite a few other rearrangements of numbers, very effective from the viewpoint of stage presentation, which have benefited the ballet as a whole.

Of course, it would be strange to justify a "rehash" of Tchaikovsky's score today. Petipa, however, could have replied to a rebuke about his revisions that no *Swan Lake* had, in effect, existed before him.

The music? The score? The scenario? Yes, probably. But not a ballet, not anything worthy of a good ballet stage at any rate.

The scenario? Well, you're welcome to read it as much as you please. Petipa created a brilliant ballet, and his production of *Swan Lake* became part and parcel of the theatrical repertoire.

Petipa's choreography was accepted as a classical version of *Swan Lake* in its own right. All later stage versions of the ballet were compared with his production rather than with Tchaikovsky's original conception. What is more, attempts to revert to the composer's original score were usually interpreted as attempts to distort his conception of the ballet.

The St. Petersburg Production

The history of the St. Petersburg production is poorly known. In his memoirs Petipa claims that he had a meeting with Tchaikovsky to discuss the plan of his future production. Musicologists, however, tend to dismiss this fact, which is plausible in itself, primarily because Petipa himself discredits it by his story about Tchaikovsky's delighted reaction to the première of *Swan Lake*, which is, of course, untrue.

Moreover, we know that Modest Tchaikovsky began revising and remaking the scenario after the composer's death. He had no instructions from his late brother to rely on, as is evidenced by the absence of any references to them in his manuscript. This fact is of crucial significance, since the new musical edition of the ballet and its choreographic plan were produced by Drigo and Petipa after the completion of the scenario.

Ivan Vesvolozhsky, Director of the Imperial Theatres, wrote in a letter to Modest Tchaikovsky (17 August, 1894) of the need to "complete the plot" of the ballet, prior to which it was impossible to get down to work on the production.

A little later this was mentioned by Drigo in his letter to Modest Tchaikovsky: "... As soon as I receive a new program, I shall go ahead with arranging musical numbers by agreement with Ivanov and Petipa."

It is clear from the foregoing that there was no definite plan of remaking *Swan Lake* in Tchaikovsky's lifetime. Neither Modest Tchaikovsky, nor Drigo, Petipa, and Ivanov had attempted to do anything to revive the ballet, so by all indications the final decision on its production was made after the composer's death.

On February 17 and 22, 1894 the second scene of *Swan Lake* in Ivanov's choreography was performed at soireés commemorating Tchaikovsky at the Marinsky Theater of St. Petersburg. Its success with the audience was evidently the main argument in favor of staging the ballet as a whole in a renovated version.

Besides, as the late Yuri Slonimsky, an eminent Soviet musicologist and dramatist, writes, "Tchaikovsky's death sent shock waves through Russian society and caused an incredible rise of interest in his music." The opera houses were sold out for every performance of his operas and ballets, and concerts of his music immediately became the focus of cultural life of St. Petersburg. Vesvolozhsky, who had earlier taken a cautious view of the idea of reviving *Swan Lake*, certainly reckoned with this upsurge of Tchaikovsky's popularity.

The revisions of *Swan Lake* were encouraged by Modest Tchaikovsky, Peter Jurgensson and Hermann Laroche, none of whom could be suspected of disrespect for the memory of the composer and his heritage. Moreover, Modest Tchaikovsky and Peter Jurgensson approved of Drigo's work on Tchaikovsky's music and never called its revisions in question. After all, they had no alternative, because the ballet could not be staged in its original version, and no choreographer would agree to run the risk of failure.

Revisions and deletions were probably an indispensable condition, and only compliance with it would guarantee a revival of the ballet on the Marinsky stage.

At the same time, both Modest Tchaikovsky and Peter Jurgensson evidently had second thoughts about the revisions in *Swan Lake*. At any rate the haste with which they tried to lend authority to innovations in the ballet suggest this idea.

For instance, Jurgensson, almost immediately after the première of 1895, issued the numbers of Tchaikovsky's 72nd piano cycle under the title *Swan Lake* and with a note saying that these numbers had been inserted into the ballet by the composer himself. It was printed in parentheses: *"Orchestration by Riccardo Drigo."*

In his biography of the composer, Modest Tchaikovsky alleged the same and included the same numbers under the rubric *Swan Lake*. Yuri Slonimsky writes reasonably that in their "style and content" these numbers were a poor fit for the score, so the composer had hardly given his consent to such inconsistent inserts.

Besides, how is one to understand the note about the inserts made by Tchaikovsky himself, if the orchestration of numbers had been made by Drigo, as was courteously acknowledged on the title page of the edition? One has to conclude that Drigo simply fulfilled the will of the late composer, who had died before he had time to orchestrate his music, having pointed out only the need to include it into *Swan Lake*. We know, however, that Drigo took up this work almost a year after the composer's death and that the problem of staging the whole ballet had not been settled with finality in Tchaikovsky's lifetime.

Marius Petipa

In 1877 when *Swan Lake* had its first night in Moscow, Petipa was 58. Though he had a long record in choreography he was still on his way to the summits of artistry. He was on the threshold of old age but his heyday in art was yet to come.

It is hard to believe that Petipa staged *The Sleeping Beauty* at the age of 70. This ballet brims with youthful energy and seems to have been created by one convinced of his everlasting life.

The majestic serenity of *The Sleeping Beauty* is the peace of wise maturity to which all pleasures of youth are accessible but without the agitation and impatience characteristic of youth.

The luxuriant palace parks, the gay-colored flower beds, the quiet of secluded corners of beautiful nature, the magic charm of mysteriously romantic caves and, all of a sudden, a merry festival in the open air or in a castle — such was the world of his ever-lasting life which defied old age and the anguish of boredom.

In that ballet, perhaps, Petipa recalled his native France so infinitely far away now. Not the romantic Paris of the 1840s, the time of his childhood and youth. His imagination called him to the Golden Age of gallantry which he resurrected on the St. Petersburg stage as a challenge to reality.

He associated with that age his worship of woman, since the gallant age was, as is known, the age of woman, when her physical and sensual beauty was idealized.

The entire art of Petipa, that genuine magician of the poetry of dance, was pervaded with joyful adoration of woman — not a mysterious beautiful stranger or a lady of romantic dreams but a wonderful toy, an item of luxury and an object of admiration, whose finest virtue is exquisite and "useless" beauty.

This was a world inhabited by fairies of diamonds and sapphires, fairies symbolizing gentleness, serenity, playfulness and daring. Faithful to the rules of the gallant age, Petipa renounced an integral image of woman; to him one appeared to be a beautiful gem, another looked like a flower, still another charmed him with innocent mischief or loving care.

Petipa's romantic mind led him to embrace the principle of natural diversity in dance. All the ballerinas who had worked under his guidance recalled his subtle instinctive feel for the natural gift of each dancer, so in choreographing a dance he was invariably guided by his unmistakable vision and never erred in choosing the right part for the right dancer.

In Petipa's ballets any dancer was always presented in the most favorable light and could demonstrate her distinctive individual merits. The dance pattern was made to fit the ballerina's own style which impressed the audience as a superlative specimen of artistry.

Petipa was not just as good at staging male dances, and in fact he did that work with a measure of reluctance. For him ballet was the realm of the fair sex, a magic fairy spectacle, a fantastic world where fairies, driads and nereids compete in grace and beauty like young ladies of noble birth, their faces concealed under mysterious masks, vie with each other at a masquerade in an exquisite salon of high society.

A male here was simply a cavalier, an escort and an onlooker graciously allowed to watch in admiration this world of refined youth and worship its beauty.

Petipa ignored old age and searched for a life of eternal bliss in this world of endless enjoyment. For him *The Sleeping Beauty* was precisely the ideal of everlasting youth embodied on stage. It was with that ideal alive in his heart that Petipa made up his mind to revive *Swan Lake* five years after the première of *The Sleeping Beauty*.

Swan Lake put Petipa in a quandary, and it was not fortuitious that he entrusted

A flower-bedecked tribute paid to Tchaikovsky's image at one of the
Tchaikovsky violin competitions.

all the main scenes of the ballet — the "swan scenes" — to Lev Ivanov. In that period Petipa certainly felt no interest in "swan romance" with its clearly dramatic and psychological message.

Odette was no longer among his heroines. Aurora and Raimonda, various fairies of diamonds and sapphires, and the characters of Charles Perrault's chivalrous fairy tales formed a circle where Odette did not belong. Petipa had banished this fairy to the past with all her ethical maximalism, sobs and fits of hysteria, her endless demands and rules of convention, and her anguish of loneliness.

The old master must have been sick and tired of that romantic nonsense, and he certainly detested the idea of returning to it, especially after his ballet experience of a blissful life in luxuriant gardens and majestic castles where the greatest drama was a sound century-old sleep. That was all of the world of *The Sleeping Beauty*.

Odile in Petipa's choreography was a far more attractive character than her melancholy double; she was a cheerful, vigorous and glamorous woman full of life and resource, who easily eclipsed and made a laughing stock of her pitiful rival — a lake Cinderella in the guise of a beautiful swan.

Odile was a Cinderella in full bloom and glamor at the Prince's ball, while Odette was a Cinderella, the plain, poor, stepdaughter doing her menial chores. The tale of Cinderella appealed very much to Petipa in general. The message of that fairy tale was unambiguous: a man's heart can be won by beauty and elegance, not by virtue hidden in rags.

Petipa mused on the tale of Cinderella and remained faithful to its moral idea as long as he lived. Indeed, was it not the elegance of dance that made him famous as the great Petipa? And was it not his inborn sense of beauty that helped him create his finest ballets?

In any event, Odile was a character consistent with Petipa's ideas and comprehensible to him, so after composing the first scene of the ballet and without making any but only a half-hearted effort to compose the third, he put all his talent and skill into the central pas de deux of Odile and Siegfried.

Competing inwardly, so to say, against Ivanov, who choreographed the wonderful pas d'action of Odette and Siegfried, Petipa had an impassioned desire of victory, not for himself, but for his heroine Odile, over her rival of the beautiful swan kingdom.

Lev Ivanov

As a choreographer Ivanov had a lyrical cast of mind and a subtle perception of music and its style first and foremost. Petipa was a "dictator" of choreography, who invariably sought to subordinate the music to his own aims. By contrast, Ivanov followed the music in search of a dance pattern close to it in plastic expression and style. This is strikingly visible in the second scene of *Swan Lake*, which has become world-famous.

In Ivanov's choreography the appearance of "swans" was preceded by pantomime episodes: Siegfried with friends (in the initial version he was accompanied by Benno and hunters) strayed off their path to the shore of Swan Lake, where they admired its mysterious sight and attempted to shoot a swan. The episode of Odette's story was also based on pantomime, and the dances began with a waltz.

The appearance of the swans conveyed an atmosphere of confusion and panic. Like a flock of birds frightened by a gunshot they dispersed all over the stage in a "zigzag pattern of the first arabesque," the tensely rhythmic waving motions of their arms expressing extreme excitement.

Little by little, the panic died down, and the swan corps de ballet lined up in what is now a famous pattern: two files stretching from the backstage to the proscenium to form a corridor adjoined by another file extending obliquely from the left flank to the audience. This composition was devoid of the conventional ballet symmetry, and the image of a "one-winged" swan depicted by it revealed the dramatic implication of the scene.

Ivanov also found his own, unorthodox avenue of approach to the music and the plot, going far beyond the limits set by a fairy tale. He did not create the image of a maiden held in captivity by witchcraft but presented an enchanted dreamy soul, sincere and emotional, timidly awakening to a fullblooded real life.

Odette is a human being who has retreated from the cruel world into her solitary refuge where she has found the desired rest and quiet.

Her sudden passion for Prince Siegfried stirs up her longing for a different (or earlier?) life and she fights for it bravely though her struggle brings her nothing but disillusionment and death.

Ivanov's Odette is a timid and defenseless being at first, before her love for Siegfried gives her courage to regain her freedom. She is not a fairy at all but an earthly maiden of flesh and blood who had found happiness in solitude and a wise and peaceful contemplation of the world of nature, the endless void of the skies and the pristine beauty of the lake waters.

Ivanov threw into sharp relief the dramatic image of Odette as a heroine of the 1890s but not of the 1870s. His Odette was closer to Shakespeare's Ophelia than to Ondine, and she had tragic knowledge of the world which had been denied to the Odette of the 1870s.

For Ivanov's Odette the earthly world was "a hateful land" of outward splendor concealing emptiness, where the air was poisoned with treachery and suspicion and where a respectable life was a veneer of vanity.

Her swan image was Odette's protest against the slavery of the ordinary world. Her magic captivity was a happy escape from the ugly monotony of the imaginary freedom of real life. Her life on the lake was a voluntary exile.

Ivanov gave his own profoundly individual interpretation of the image of Odette as a symbol of a woman's lonely fate, as a proud and withdrawn swan maiden who embodies the tragic helplessness of goodness in the face of human perfidy and magic evil. The choreographer dramatized that image by lending it a shade of pessimism, not grimness but elegiac lyricism in the spirit of the poetry of his time pervaded with a motif of withdrawal from the world and a collapse of lofty life ideals overpowered by cruelty, hypocrisy and deceit.

The Swan Suite

In *The Swan Suite* Ivanov laid down a new principle of relationship between the corps de ballet and the hero. The swan corps de ballet is not simply a group of Odette's companions or a decorative backdrop for the love story developing in front of it.

This is an image of her thoughts and emotions, her inner lyrical "voice." Therefore, we cannot describe the swan corps de ballet as a dramatic personage in its own right with its own biography, destiny and character, and its own functions in the action.

The whole second scene of the ballet was composed by Ivanov acting, as it were, in the first person, on behalf of Odette, delivering her inner monologue, her confession and her story keynoted by her distinctive sensation of events.

This monologue is interrupted only once, by the dialogue-adagio with Siegfried, but this episode, too, is colored by the heroine's subjective perceptions.

The swan corps de ballet is a personified metaphor of Odette's swan image rather than a group of concrete images of her betwitched maiden friends. This is an image of Odette's swan destiny, her "swan plumage," the embodiment of her secret sorrow and her "swan soul" in Akim Volynsky's phrase.

This swan corps de ballet has not and cannot have a personal drama and conflict of its own; it simply reflects the lyrical world of the heroine. The swan corps de ballet is a brilliant invention of Lev Ivanov.

Just as in the ballet score the swan suite was opened by a waltz. Besides a corps de ballet of adult dancers and soloists, eight ballet pupils dancing little swans took part in this scene. In today's productions this group of eight children is absent.

As in the *Waltz of Flowers* in *The Sleeping Beauty*, where children were also included in the cast, the image of childhood was compared here with the image of youth, since the world of Odette, just as, incidentally, that of Princess Aurora in the first act of the ballet, is one of transition from childhood to maidenhood.

It will be recalled that in the ballet plot Odette is 16 or 17, which is a fairly important detail. Indeed, describing *The Nutcracker* as a choreographic poem of childhood on the verge of vague premonitions of youth, as the musicologist Boris Asafiev put it, we tend to forget that Tchaikovsky's two first ballets are dedicated, in effect, to the same theme.

Siegfried and Odette, Aurora and Desire are all very young heroes on the threshold of first love and first experiences that shape their moral and ethical outlook on the world.

In the libretto of 1877 this motif was quite conspicuous: the world of Odette was one of youthful fun and naiveté where any sophistication would seem irrelevant.

In the 1870s Tchaikovsky was fascinated with that theme. Let us recall the characters of his music of that period: the Snow Maiden, Miranda, Ondine...and, finally, Romeo and Juliet,"...youngsters absorbed in the delights of shared love who find themselves in a tragic and hopeless situation." This phrase of Tchaikovsky's holds true of the two loving hearts in *Swan Lake* as well.

It is true, Pavel Herdt, who danced the part of Prince Siegfried in the St. Petersburg production, was hardly able to convey the spirit of youth as well as he had done it at a younger age. He was almost fifty at the time.

Dancers, of course, always impart something of their own interpretation to both the theme and conception of a ballet.

Pierina Legnani, the prima ballerina of the Marinsky Theater, who was the first to dance Odette on the St. Petersburg stage, looks from photographs as a graceful and youthful but fully mature woman in the prime of life.

For all that Ivanov's choreography gave vent to the sentiments of youth which are audible in the music, lending it the sincerity and ardor of first love emotions.

The waltz of the swans presented the world of Odette and served as a prelude to the first meeting — adagio — of Siegfried and Odette.

The choreographer confined the duet to a very narrow space; it was, in fact, a dance in a small spot of the stage like the singing of an aria in an opera where the singer stands still, addressing the audience and the partner.

Almost the whole adagio was open to view from the front, and profile positions were taking only in supports, with brief and swift leaps preserving the main pattern of arabesque, the leitmotif of the duet.

The swan corps de ballet filled the pauses in developing the dance composition and not so much accompanied the leading parts as expressed Odette's emotions; the dance of the corps de ballet was the poetic implication of the scene expressing her misgivings and anxiety.

The adagio of Siegfried and Odette was followed by the dances of swans. The world of Odette was laid open to Prince Siegfried.

This world had a merry side shown by the dance of little swans playing pranks and being naughty like children.

The dance of large swans expressed the freedom-loving spirit of this world and its independent and proud youth.

The suite was crowned by Odette's variations, a monologue of loneliness with intonations of childlike grace, naive lyrical dreams and a longing for flight held in check by captivity and witchcraft.

The swan suite threw into salient relief Ivanov's talent as a symphonist choreographer. There were just a few episodes here: the first meeting, mutual explanations, and parting. That was a novella about a mysterious stranger. One meeting with her was enough to overturn the life of an easy-going young man.

The dance extended the episodes of the plot and led them into the sphere of poetry.

Yuri Grigorovich said in this context, referring to Ivanov's brilliant contributions to ballet:

"His artistic interpretation of the swan suite in dance influenced tremendously the succeeding generations of choreographers. He invented the principle of interaction between the hero and the corps de ballet and the principle of its poetic personification, both of which lie at the basis of the artistic structure of ballets staged by modern choreographers."

Yuri Grigorovich

The Black Swans

A corps de ballet of black swans dancing the waltz opening the final scene was another innovation in the St. Petersburg production. This idea evidently belonged to Petipa, as is evidenced by his rough notes and drawings illustrating his work on the fourth scene.

The black swans did not come on stage at once; in the choreographic plan of the waltz the corps de ballet of white swans formed a triangle with its top facing the stage front in a mise en scène familiar from the second scene.

Then the corps de ballet dispersed to both sides and started to dance a pensive and melancholy waltz, although in its color and mood this episode had no sombre intonations.

This composition had a touch of sadness and idyll, and even the appearance of black swans did not disturb its strange harmony. The white swans had no foreboding of disaster; they were a little excited and surprised by Odette's disappearance, but were quietly waiting for her return.

A motif of inevitable misfortune, however, was imperatively forcing its way into their peaceful and elegiac dance. The swan maidens had no implicit faith in the freedom of the carefree world any longer. Black swans portending doom and catastrophe had invaded it. They cut through the corps de ballet of white swans, imitated their motions, circled over the stage, drew up ranks, now girdling groups of white swans lined up along the stage edge, now moving to the stage center.

A group of white swans advancing on the audience was suddenly followed by a group of black swans; a line followed a line, light and shade, snow-white and black tutus changed in rapid succession to create an image of beauty humiliated and betrayed.

The dance, however, remained harmonious and staid. It seemed that a strange friendship and a strange community of feeling linked the swan maidens with their sinister black doubles.

Goodness retreated before evil, hope gave way to despair, joy resigned itself to misfortune. The black swans were unhappy and anguished like their white sisters, and shared their grief at the loss of the world of childhood and innocent youth destroyed by the treachery of human love.

The black swans were Ivanov and Petipa's brilliant discovery.

The St. Petersburg production had a tragic finale: Siegfried and Odette committed suicide. At first glance, this end of the ballet had no psychological motivation. Indeed, Rothbart did not appear on stage in the swan scenes, and the lake was not disturbed by a violent storm at Vsevolozhsky's request. So there was no visible motive for the heroes' decision to take their lives.

Nevertheless, the events of the ballet led to a tragic dènouement. Modest Tchaikovksy imparted an element of fatal inevitability to the finale to reveal the theme of love and death which had not existed either in the production or the scenario of 1877.

In the St. Petersburg production of 1895 Siegfried and Odette decide to die rather than part forever; they know that happiness is unattainable. The motif of the tragic helplessness of good before evil was the keynote of the message of the ballet.

It is true, the production culminated in what Yuri Slonimsky described as a "vulgar apotheosis" with nymphs and naiads welcoming Odette and Siegfried to their underwater kingdom.

That apotheosis was not without its meaning, however. The music called for an optimistic resolution of the final scene in a major tone. The authors of the new version could not conclude the ballet with a scene of swans swimming on the lake. That would have contradicted their conception of the plot in which the theme of a storm purifying and renovating life was absent.

The "vulgar apotheosis" invented by Modest Tchaikovksy was consistent, nevertheless, with the new conception, one of "a blissful life of eternity in the next world." That dènouement did not deprive the ballet of its tragic appeal but was consonant with the music in its optimistic spirit, though that consonance was, of course, simply formal.

Summing Up

Petipa and Ivanov's production lacked artistic integrity, of course. Their new conception was fulfilled only in the swan scenes, while the first and the third scenes remained within the limits of a traditional ball-like performance. The superior achievement in the choreography of the third scene was the famous pas de deux of Siegfried and Odile, a masterpiece of art created by Petipa.

Fedor Lopukhov, a famous Soviet choreographer, described this pas de deux as a duet, having in mind its basis in the plot, and he was certainly right. That was, in effect, a perfectly new and special type of pas de deux, not a run-of-the-mill dance number intended to delight the audience with superlative virtuosity but a dramatic duet with its own theme and psychological message.

In the pas de deux of Odile and Siegfried, Petipa made skilful and subtle use of the plastic dance motifs of the swan adagio as if to make a parody of its positions. The adagio of Odette and Siegfried was a veritable song adagio, a cantilena of softly flowing movements creating the effect of a continually developing dance melody.

The duet of Odile and Siegfried followed a sharp rhythmic pattern. Odile was a seductive and mysterious stranger luring the Prince with every movement of her broad and sensual dance. The plastic pattern of her arms resembled the movements of Odette the swan, but this likeness had a sinister, treacherous and predatory nuance.

The pas de deux of Odile and Siegfried was one of Petipa's finest achievements. On the whole, however, the third scene hardly deserved to be praised. The musical dramaturgy had quite a few flaws. Revising the score at his discretion, Petipa has sought to produce a divertissement spectacle.

The version of 1895 completed the short and dramatic history of productions of *Swan Lake* in the 19th century. The stage history of this ballet in the 20th century, however, also began from Petipa and Ivanov's version.

The point is not that the finest fragments of their version have survived to date. All the choreographers of the 20th century who staged *Swan Lake* relied on the production of 1895, continuing its traditions, or challenging them, or trying to integrate them with the modern trends in the development of ballet.

Choreographer
Yuri Grigorovich

Choreographer
Marius Petipa

Choreographer
Lev Ivanov

Choreographer
Alexander Gorsky

Designer
Simon Virsaladze

PRINCE SIEGFRIED

Mikhail Mordkin.
1901.

Alexander Volinin.
1908.

Lavrenty Novikov.
1910.

Victor Smoltsov.
1920.

Asaf Messerer.
1922.

Vladimir Preobrazhensky.
1943.

Nikolai Fadeyechev.
1954.

Maris Liepa.
1961.

Valery Anisimov.
1977.

The Homecoming

In the early 20th century *Swan Lake* came back to the Moscow stage. In 1901 the choreographer Alexander Gorsky revived the ballet at the Bolshoi. That production was the first in the stage history of *Swan Lake* in the present century.

In fact, the version of 1901 cannot be considered an original one. Gorsky relied on Petipa and Ivanov's production without infringing its artistic and dramaturgical conception. He limited his intervention to editing the St. Petersburg production.

Fascinated by the experiments of the Art Theater, which were in vogue at the time, Gorsky went out of his way to plan the action of the ballet in a simple, logical and psychologically motivated manner to achieve a stylistic interpretation faithful to the style of the historical epoch revived in his production.

The production of 1895 had none of such merits, so Gorsky, while preserving the finest dance scenes invented by Petipa and Ivanov, sought to find a novel stage setting and artistic style for them.

In the course of a few years, while the production was in the repertoire, Gorsky continued his work to bring it to perfection, as he viewed it, of course.

In its final form, Gorsky's version differed significantly from the St. Petersburg production. The first act of the ballet and individual episodes in the third act were practically choreographed anew. Numerous revisions were also made in the swan scenes, which lost in Gorsky's version their austere academic harmony, integrity and consummate pattern.

In 1920 Gorsky made an attempt to produce an original stage version of Tchaikovsky's ballet. Taking advantage of what he had found in the earlier versions, he resolutely broke with the traditions of the St. Petersburg production of 1895, both in his interpretation of the subject and in the choreography.

In fact, practically nothing of Petipa and Ivanov's choreography survived in Gorsky's new production. For all his efforts to enhance the dramatic, social and genre elements in the ballet, however, Gorsky's experiment failed to impress favorably either the ballet company or the audience.

In 1922, therefore, the choreographer revived his earlier version which was consistent with the prevailing interpretation of Tchaikovsky's music. Incidentally, a few innovations made in the production of 1920 were retained.

They were also used in the production of *Swan Lake* which had been in the Bolshoi repertoire until recently. That was a version of 1937 created on the basis of Gorsky's last production with the fourth act in a new choreography of Asaf Messerer.

Such is a general chronicle of Gorsky's work on *Swan Lake*. None of the 20th-century choreographers turned their attention to this ballet as often as he did.

Many historians of the art of ballet qualify Gorsky's experiments with *Swan Lake* as very unsuccessful and absolutely unwarranted. There is a grain of truth in their judgment. Indeed, none of Gorsky's versions could stand comparison with Petipa and Ivanov's production which has come to be regarded as classical.

Nevertheless, Gorsky's productions were not lost to posterity, but suggested ideas taken up and developed in the versions of Agrippina Vaganova and Fedor Lopukhov, and in the Moscow version of Vladimir Burmeister, who for his part exerted a certain influence on Yuri Grigorovich's interpretation of *Swan Lake*.

In other words, all of the most interesting versions of *Swan Lake* in the 20th century are linked to a varying extent with Gorsky's experiments. Already in his first versions of *Swan Lake*, prior to 1920, he had sought to dramatize the events in the ballet and to sharpen the conflict between dreams and reality intrinsic to its message.

The choreographer gave keen attention to the first act, which had been a failure on the whole in the St. Petersburg production of 1895. In contrast to Petipa who had attached no great significance to the first scene of the ballet, Gorsky strove to create the image of the world of Prince Siegfried.

Critics immediately noted the merits of the first scene in Gorsky's choreography. Comparing his version with that of Petipa, they expressed themselves in favor of Gorsky's production, emphasizing its more picturesque effects and more meaningful message.

Gorsky also sought to lend medieval colors to the action. This was imitated by all later choreographers of the ballet. There was a ball in medieval style in Vaganova's version; Lopukhov reinforced the image of Rothbart with the paraphernalia of knighthood; and Grigorovich's version conveys the atmosphere of a medieval legend.

Tchaikovsky and Grigorovich

Before his production of *Swan Lake* Grigorovich had some experience of work on Tchaikovsky's ballet music. In 1963 the choreographer revived *The Sleeping Beauty* in Petipa's choreography at the Bolshoi and three years later produced his own version of *The Nutcracker*.

His work on this ballet meant a great deal for his future production of *Swan Lake*. In the context of his practical assimilation of the classical tradition and the choreographic principles of the 19th-century ballet theater *The Sleeping Beauty* and *The Nutcracker* were among Grigorovich's first productions in Moscow in the early period of his work as a choreographer when his own method and aesthetic creed were in their formative stage.

That period culminated in the production of *Spartacus* in 1968, a ballet that summed up the results of the first decade of his work as a choreographer. It was followed by *Swan Lake*, which was in a way a milestone on his path from his early productions to *Ivan the Terrible* and *Romeo and Juliet*.

In his first version of *The Sleeping Beauty* produced in 1963 the choreographer learned the specific world of Petipa's imagery and the laws of symphonic dance. Already in that production he had tried many methods he would later use.

In *The Sleeping Beauty* the choreographer had renounced genre pantomime traditional in classical ballet, that is, the division of dance into classical and character dances. *The Sleeping Beauty* was choreographed in a uniform key, in classical style.

That was perhaps the first experiment of this kind in the history of choreographic art. Grigorovich continued this experiment in *The Nutcracker* and then in *Swan Lake*: the ethnic dances of the divertissement in both ballets are devised as classical miniatures with a view to the excellent point technique of the soloists.

In addition, in *The Sleeping Beauty* Grigorovich tried out some of his novel composition ideas on large choreographic ensembles.

Thus, unlike his predecessors, with the exception of Petipa, choreographers who had staged *Swan Lake*, Grigorovich got down to work on this ballet after a period of association with Tchaikovsky's music, which had been fairly intensive at that.

No such experience was available to Gorsky, who undertook to stage *Swan Lake* at a very early stage of his career in choreography. Nor was it available to Vaganova, Burmeister and Lopukhov.

Grigorovich was in a favorable situation, since Tchaikovsky's music held a conspicuous place in his art and not only in his Moscow productions of *The Sleeping Beauty* and *The Nutcracker*.

Yuri Grigorovich

In the season of 1962-1963 Grigorovich was the art director of a new version of *Swan Lake* staged at the Novosibirsk Opera House. Petipa and Ivanov's classical version had provided the guidelines for that production, but already in it Grigorovich had attempted to come up with a new interpretation of Evil Genius.

A Crucial Decision

Starting his work on *Swan Lake* in 1968, Grigorovich at first pursued very modest and simply practical aims. He was to renew the production that was in the Bolshoi repertoire at the time. Its art direction and stage setting were in need of renovation and its choreography demanded partial revisions.

That renewal was not dictated by the choreographer's ambitions or the Bolshoi management. In fact, *Swan Lake* which had always been a central item in the Bolshoi repertoire was a strange and tasteless spectacle, and its life was sustained only by a few outstanding dancers.

Technically it was listed among Gorsky's productions, but almost nothing, in effect, remained of the choreographer's original conception: the action had lost its distinctive tonality of style, the dramatic expressiveness of mise en scènes, the exquisite quality of stage setting, and the general medieval colors of the events, that is, all the components of the choreography Gorsky regarded as crucial to his interpretation of *Swan Lake*.

That pompous production had many absurdities, such as cardboard swans and the senseless final scuffle between Siegfried and Evil Genius, who had one of his wings torn off by the hero to the thunderous accompaniment of the brasses. "Evil" was writhing in agony on the stage floor, while "Good" was solemnly uplifting its arms with the look of a circus magician who had performed a clever trick. The sun was rising over the lake, promising a new life to the swans.

The idea of a radical revision of the traditional version of *Swan Lake* was not born overnight. Grigorovich arrived at it slowly in the process of studying the history of *Swan Lake* and Tchaikovsky's music. It was the music that spurred his fantasy and stimulated his quest of a new approach to *Swan Lake*. His fascination with the theme of the ballet encouraged him to go beyond the limits of the restoration work he had initially planned to do.

A Painful Dilemma

One of the best merits of Grigorovich's artistic method is his imaginative use of past experience and wisely balanced attitude to tradition and innovation. He respects tradition but he defies it when he is firmly confident that it has exhausted itself.

As is known, breaking is easier than making things, and Grigorovich never forgets this simple truism. Adulation of the brilliant past is alien to his nature, but he despises a vandalic attitude to it, and is cautious in evaluating the traditional concepts and carefully examines their genuineness.

Grigorovich regarded as his first duty the fullest possible restoration of the composer's score, not so much the order of its numbers as the tempos and orchestration, as well as the revealing of the deletions made by former choreographers of the ballet.

He formulated this task without any reservations, although its practical implementation definitely required them. He was determined from the start to preserve Ivanov's swan scene and the famous pas de deux of Odile and Siegfried invented by Petipa.

As is known, the classics of the ballet theater had handled the music very freely in both these cases, so Grigorovich found himself in a quandary.

He was very concerned about the integrity of his future production, which was to incorporate fragments from different versions of the ballet and to be brought as close to the music as possible. After a long reflection, however, he found a way out of his dilemma.

Prince Siegfried

Grigorovich attached special significance to the first scene of the ballet as the source of the dramatic conflict in the ballet as a whole.

The first scene was a dance festival. The medieval atmosphere was felt immediately when four trumpeters in heavy, richly ornamented garb appeared in the opening scene. The semi-circular curtain of the proscenium stretched across the stage center was emblazoned with heraldic bearings. Another ancient-looking curtain was used in the swan scenes, in the finale of the first act, and in the scene of seduction at the ball. A poetic image of the swan was depicted on it.

The two curtains symbolized the two spheres of the hero's life: the official and the intimate.

Peter Ilich Tchaikovsky towards the close of his life.

These curtains, in the choreographer's conception, were to demarcate the two different areas of the action in which fantasy and reality were so closely intermingled that the boundary between them was almost imperceptible.

The scene of conferring knighthood on Prince Siegfried was very important for the general message of the act. The hero performed a solemn ritual prescribed by the time-honored traditions of chivalry and took an oath of allegiance to his knightly duty of service of the noble cause preordained by his noble birth.

The four heralds who blew their trumpets to announce the opening of the festival and the entrées of noble guests symbolized this ritual custom and the idea of a fatal encounter between duty and freedom.

As the festival drew to a close Prince Siegfried was seized with vague anxiety. He ascended to the castle gallery, stared intently into the distance, passed between the rows of dancers with a look of concern and absorption in some secret thoughts on his face.

The stage quickly sank into dimness, and only the golden goblets in the hands of the Prince's friends glistened mysteriously. Night was coming, and his friends vanished in its dark blue shadows, leaving him alone with his thoughts.

The theme of the lake was coming on and its emblem on a curtain descended from the darkness of night. Siegfried's dance assumed lyrical intonations, his motions and poses were now cautious and expectant, unlike the previous scenes of virtuoso dance in which solemnity and ceremony had prevailed.

His plastic poses were reminiscent of a swan as his spectacular leaps and turns were followed by arabesques and cantilena-like flowing combinations of movements.

At the point of culmination of the swan theme with the whole orchestra sounding powerfully Evil Genius came on the scene and stood still behind Siegfried's back. Grigorovich had composed a long duet of Siegfried and Rothbart to the music of the orchestral introduction to the second scene.

Destiny seemed to be in pursuit of the hero, setting the pace of his movements, and Siegfried's dance imitated the dance of his adversary. Rothbart's dance also exhibited swan-like movements, particularly in the motions of his arms, which did not imitate the flapping of a swan's wings but bore a sinister resemblance to them distorted by black magic.

On the whole, the duet created an image of escape to the lake, a flight from the black evil shadow of destiny pointing the way towards the swan kingdom.

A New Version of the Swan Suite

Grigorovich preserved in his choreography Odette's variations, pas a'action, the dance of little swans and the coda from Ivanov's swan suite. The dance of large swans was left in as it was in Gorsky's choreography, just as the entrance of the corps de ballet — an anxious and dramatically confused run in a circle.

In his editing of the classical fragments he took care not to impair the details of their dance language. While leaving the pattern and combinations of movements intact, however, Grigorovich tried to avoid imitativeness in the plastic motions of the arms.

He preferred a more graphic and sharper pattern to a simple imitation of swan movements so as to lend the whole scene a different stylistic tonality. In his choreography the swans were characters from the fantastic world of fairies, enchanted princesses, whose plastic dance was slightly stylized but never naturalistic.

In this scene Grigorovich continued the development of the main conflict between Siegfried and Rothbart. All the scenes before the great waltz of swans had been pervaded with dramatic conflicts. After Odette's entrance Rothbart vanished, but he reappeared at the end of his story about her lot, and stealthily sneaked up to Siegfried and Odette, as the music developed the theme of fate pursuing the heroine.

Grigorovich had composed a dramatic dance trio for this episode. Rothbart vehemently tried to ruin the union of Siegfried and Odette, and his figure now and then emerged in their way, the lines of the dance patterns diverged from the stage center and converged upon it again, as though a violent gust of wind threw them away from each other until finally Rothbart forced Odette to withdraw.

Siegfried attempted to follow her, but Rothbart standing behind him stepped back as though pulling the Prince backwards by a magnetic force. Siegfried's dance showed his effort to overcome this magic power, and he extended his arms towards Odette, but his body obeyed Rothbart's will.

The Prince exhausted by this hopeless struggle fell to his knees, but Rothbart again appeared behind his back and forced him to stand up as though holding him in his embrace.

Overpowered but unsubdued, Siegfried was wrestling with this black vice of destiny, his body feeling weak and limp and his arms raised in a grievous lament but suddenly, by the last desperate effort, he wrested himself free of Rothbart's deadly embrace. The magician showed him the way to Odette with treacherous courtesy.

The next moment swans swarmed the stage at a signal given by Rothbart, and the ball dance of first love began. In the finale of the act the swan theme continued in the music, Rothbart appeared again; Odette vanished from the scene, a coat of arms descended to the stage to separate the heroes, and the sinister black figure of destiny again emerged behind Siegfried.

The Brides

Grigorovich had intended to restore for a start the central scene of the ball act, a large dance suite in which the conflict attains its culmination. At the same time, he was compelled to retain the pas de deux composed by Petipa, having found new variations for it instead of the female variation insert to the music of Tchaikovsky's piano piece and the male variations that Drigo had borrowed from available material. Moreover, Grigorovich had to determine the place and content of the national divertissement dances.

Grigorovich came up with his own principle of staging divertissement dances which influenced the dramaturgical structure and content of the action.

"The brides as a divertissement, that is, all divertissement dances mean the arrival of the brides. This is danced by different brides...All dance in classical style," he wrote in his rough notes for the production.

Thus he arrived at the idea of a divertissement as a component of the general suite of the brides crowned with a great classical waltz.

Every national dance became an entrèe performance of one of the brides, each of whom represented a distinctive type of temperament rather than a concrete national character. Therefore, the traditional tap dances were remade into classical ones.

The dances of the brides were choreographed as solo variations with active accompaniment of the corps de ballet — the retinue of a bride. The costumes of the brides in national style were basically identical ball-dresses of a pale yellow color.

Later, when rehearsals were already in progress, Grigorovich added a fifth, Russian, dance to the four dances of the divertissement, so that the waltz of the brides assumed the form of a peculiar pas de six (five brides and Siegfried), that is, almost what had been intended by Tchaikovsky in his time.

This plan of the divertissement lent the action an integral dramaturgical line and a through theme — the choice of a bride. Odile was the sixth bride at the ball; Odette would become the seventh — a tragic misfit at this love and treachery contest.

The totally new and original choreography of the divertissement was among Grigorovich's finest achievements in this production.

Seduction

The entrèe of Rothbart and Odile was choreographed as a virtuoso dynamic dance which immediately added a mysterious infernal note to the action. The dance was the beginning of witchcraft, the stage lights dimmed to semi-darkness, the curtain emblazoned with armorial bearings descended to the floor, and Odile stopped in front of it in the stage center and was immediately surrounded by black swans.

The trio of "seduction" in which Odile appeared before Siegfried in the image of a swan for the first time developed individual dance motifs of Ivanov's adagio from the second scene.

Odile was acting out her sham tragic love and tragic destiny, appealing for sympathy and compassion, pleading for help and trying to infatuate the Prince not with the charms of her beauty but with her bitter tears and supplication.

Grigorovich had discerned the psychological message of the music in which the song of a suffering swan sounds like the tragic call of destiny hastening the onset of disaster, like the incantations of evil magic that deceive a trustful victim not by spectacular visual effects but by moving his heart.

Love was the only alternative to death. Love was her only hope, and Odile acted in front of Siegfried the tragic end of her life, pretending to die on his hands, and their duet was his dance with a dying innocent maiden.

Odile's limp body sank down in his arms, her arms fell listlessly, and her face was a mask of death. The vision of his dying beloved wounded his heart and forced him to make a quick decision.

Their dance was based on contrasts of different motifs: the leaps of Odile-Odette with Siegfried's supports and the leaps of a triumphant Rothbart who was again, just as at the lake, pursuing and watching them.

Here, Rothbart caught Odile-Odette in the air, as if wresting her from Siegfried's embrace, and dictated his will to him, now appearing in the image of a powerful magician ruling his destiny, now looking like his fortunate rival leading Odile away gently and treacherously.

In the finale of the trio the malicious design of evil magic forces materialized in a scene where Siegfried knelt before Odile standing in an arabesque. Odile bent over him slightly and stretched out her arms which were immediately seized by Rothbart standing behind his back.

The Denouement

Composing the fourth scene of *Swan Lake* anew, Grigorovich took account of the experience of its different earlier versions. The point of departure in his quests of the best choreographic solution, however, was Ivanov's compositions.

It was on their dance motifs that Grigorovich based his choreographic score of rare musicality, which bears a clear imprint of his genuine symphonic thinking. The fourth scene was indisputably the best in the production for its integral and dynamic character.

The culmination of the act was the scene of a storm on the lake invoked by Rothbart; the peals of thunder accompanied his virtuoso demoniac leaps.

The swan corps de ballet performed new functions in this scene: running between the heroes, the swans tried to keep them apart and break up their union and then to hide Odette from Siegfried.

The storm was the poetical image of the troubled emotions of the heroes. The swan corps de ballet seemed to implore them to part, anticipating disaster, and would not let Odette join in the encounter between Siegfried and Rothbart going on in front of them.

At the same time, the dance of the swans expressed the heroes' anguish and suffering. It was the image of a lake of tears overflowing its shores, the image of nature torn by a storm and protesting against violence. Each of the heroes was encircled by swans of the corps de ballet and vainly tried to break the spell of the forces fettering their will.

Odette did not and could not forgive Siegfried: his mistake had brought into play the law of destiny embodied by the ruler of the storm — Rothbart.

Odette was unable to forgive Siegfried but her heart went out to him. Her love alone could save his life. They freed themselves of the deadly waves and flew towards each other but at this instant the formidable figure of the evil magician rose between them.

In the first variant of Grigorovich's version Rothbart carried by a violent wind flew between Odette and Siegfried, and she fell into his embrace, lifeless. Rothbart, the devil expelled from the soul, vanished in the castle flooded by the lake waters. The swans approached the dying Odette, the tremulous motions of their arms conveying a motif of Nature appeased. The corps de ballet slowly withdrew into darkness. Odette was prostrate in the stage center, and a curtain bearing the emblem of a swan slowly fell between her and Siegfried.

The curtain separated them forever, and Odette's body was raised aloft slowly as though it soared into the sky. Siegfried fell on his knee and took an oath of allegiance to his ideal.

Later Grigorovich revised this finale. Odette spread her arms to protect Siegfried against Rothbart, and the hero swore faithfulness to his beloved. Rothbart wriggled in impotent fury and died before the eyes of the heroes exulting in their victory.

The sun was rising over the lake. Love triumphed over death.

This photograph of a pensive Tchaikovsky was taken late in his life.

CONCLUSION

Yuri Grigorovich's version of *Swan Lake* has had a happy life on stage. This is the finest version of *Swan Lake* in today's repertoire.

"Nevertheless," the choreographer says, "it can be remade into a totally new production. Working on *Swan Lake* I seem to feel a shade of dissatisfaction with myself. At first glance everything looks good but after a time I see a flaw here and a flaw there...In short, this is a treacherous work very much like Odile herself."

In Grigorovich's production the leading parts are danced by the most celebrated soloists. For a long time the part of Odette-Odile was invariably danced by Maya Plisetskaya.

The image of Odette-Odile in Natalie Bessmertnova's interpretation is generally regarded as a milestone in the history of dance.

Of the younger ballerinas Lyudmila Semenyaka and Nina Ananiashvili are attracting much public interest now.

Swan Lake is, of course, the ballet of a lifetime for a ballerina. The part of Prince Siegfried, however, has also seen quite a few vivid interpretations in the past years. In the première of 1969 it was danced by Nikolai Fadeyechev, and today his son Alexander is reputedly the best.

Other brilliant male dancers are Alexander Bogatyrev, Yuri Vasyuchenko, and Irek Mukhamedov.

"And still, I may be willing to stage *Swan Lake* again," says Yuri Grigorovich, whose present version has summed up a long and eventful period in the history of this great ballet.

SWAN LAKE

A ballet in three acts (four scenes)

SYNOPSIS

ACT I. *Scene 1*. Prince Siegfried has come of age. It is a happy but disturbing day, for he must now accept the responsibilities of manhood and his position as ruler. The first to congratulate him are the court jester and his old tutor. His own friends follow, and after them all the people of the castle. Vassals of the prince arrive from distant lands. They present him with a sword and a knight's cross, symbols of his sovereignty over them, and swear an oath of allegiance to his mother, the ruling Princess, for help and counsel. The magnificent celebrations continue, while the Prince withdraws, longing to be alone.

Scene 2. The Lakeside. Rothbart, an Evil Magician, has bewitched young girls and transformed them into white swans. Only if some man truly loves the most beautiful of them, Odette, can the spell be broken and Rothbart's power be destroyed. Siegfried comes to the shore of the lake. He sees Odette—transfixed by her beauty and her sad fate, he is overcome by feelings of compassion and tenderness. As the Evil Magician drives the swans from the shore, Siegfried bids farewell to Odette, vowing to return and free her from the evil spell.

ACT II. The Ballroom. To strengthen his position as a ruler, Siegfried must choose a bride. Amid splendid festivities, princesses from Hungary, Spain, Russia, Naples and Poland are presented to him. But none pleases him, as he has given his love to Odette. Suddenly a stranger enters escorting a princess, Odile, who closely resembles Odette. Casting a spell on Siegfried, the stranger lures him into mistaking the mysterious princess for his Swan Queen. But in the end Siegfried feels that Odile is false, and he recognizes the stranger as the Evil Magician. Siegfried rejects Odile.

ACT III. The Lakeside. The swans are distraught. If Siegfried has broken his vow, they are doomed to remain under Rothbart's spell forever. In the middle of a great storm Siegfried rushes in, searching for Odette. Despite all his efforts to hide Odette, Rothbart cannot stop the youth in whose heart true love has been born. The magic of the Evil Magician has been broken by the power of human love . . .

It is supposed to be a happy day as Prince Siegfried comes of age and prepares to assume the throne. All of the Prince's subjects are there and he has been presented with a ceremonial sword which symbolizes his newly acquired power. How proud is the prince! For now he is a man . . . and a powerful man at that. But deep within his breast is a sad feeling which he fails to understand.

But so happy are his friendly subjects who love Prince Siegfried so much, that spontaneous boisterous dancing breaks out with everyone taking part in the joyous festivities. In magnificent and colorful costumes, wonderful skillful partners take turns in showing off their dancing skills in honor of Prince Siegfried.

The most beautiful maidens do everything possible to entice Siegfried to dance with them . . . but Siegfried seems preoccupied.

Sensing this seriousness, the Court Jester suddenly springs forward. He is always alert to such happenings and he is skillful in making everybody laugh and forget their troubles.

His playfulness catches on ... more and more people start to dance ... the mood of the people in the castle suddenly changes and everyone is happy once again.

Siegfried's friends surround him on all sides, begging him to join in the celebration, showing their love and respect for him . . . proving their willingness to do anything that will make him happy.

Since Prince Siegfried will soon become their King, they all swear to the heavens that they will forever be loyal to him and serve him in any way that he may wish.

The Knights raise their goblets to toast the Long Life of the King . . . everyone is so happy that their new ruler, Prince Siegfried, is so young, handsome, honest and kind. The drinking of the symbolic wine signals the beginning of a great feast.

As the feast reaches its climax, the Prince begins to iso-
late himself and finally withdraws from the celebration
and leaves the castle. So quietly and discreetly does he
leave, that no one notices.

Siegfried longs for the privacy of his own thoughts. The huge responsibility is awesome. Is he good enough to be a King? He comes to a quiet, desolate lake, just the perfect place to reflect upon his fate . . .

... suddenly, as if by magic, the lake comes alive with beautiful swans. They are represented by beautiful dancing girls dressed in swan-white costumes. Their gracefulness overwhelms the Prince.

How skillful are these magnificent swans . . . how disci-
plined is their dancing . . . So perfect is their behavior that
one wonders if some special power prevails over their every movement . . . the Prince becomes enthralled.

Suddenly the Swan Maidens begin their tale of woe. The story is so sad that they slowly turn from a great happy, frenzied joy, to the sober reality of perpetual bondage.

The story continues
... Rothbart, an evil
magician, has
bewitched certain
beautiful young girls
and transformed
them into lovely
white swans. They all
live together in The
Swan Lake. Only
during the night are
they allowed to come
to the lake and
become themselves
again ... but with
the first rays of dawn,
they all instantly turn
back into swans.

Suddenly the most beautiful Swan Maiden of all . . . Odette, the Swan Queen, presents herself. She alone can free the other Swan Maidens.

To destroy Rothbart's considerable power and to break the spell, someone must fall in love with Odette and prove, unconditionally, his faithfulness to her.

Siegfried is touched deeply by the plight of the Swan Maidens. His own troubles quickly disappear . . .

And he immediately falls in love with the Swan Queen and her delicate, lovely beauty. She is everything he ever dreamed of in a wife.

While Siegfried tells Odette of his love at first sight, she doesn't dare believe in the sincerity of his feelings. How could a real Prince fall in love at first sight, she thinks.

Siegfried is overwhelmed first, by the disappearance of his own depression, and then by the wonderful feelings of love and admiration he has for the Swan Queen Odette. He pleads with her repeatedly to entrust her life to him. He promises to free her and the other Swan Maidens if she will only promise to love him in return . . . for love will conquer all.

Odette swears
her trust in
Siegfried. Yes,
she loves him
too.

"My life is in your hands," cries Odette. "Please don't fail me, for if you do I will be doomed forever under the spell of this terrible magician called Rothbart." The Prince continues to pledge his love and protection.

Fascinated by Odette's beauty and grace ... and the great mystery that surrounds her, Siegfried accepts the challenge as his first duty as King. He pledges that his love will be strong enough to overcome the spell of Rothbart ... he is strong enough ... and powerful enough ... to destroy Rothbart and his evil curses. Odette and her friends will soon be free.

Dawn is approaching . . . the sky is getting lighter. "I must leave," says Odette. "Please remember your vows of love, for I shall repeat mine to myself over and over again." All the Swan Maidens dance forward, begging Prince Siegfried to keep his promises, for he is their only hope of freedom from an eternity of imprisonment. "Have no fear," says the Prince. "I shall seek out Rothbart immediately and destroy him."

Meanwhile, the celebrations at the castle have continued since no one realized that Siegfried had slipped away. The climax of the celebration is the presentation of potential brides for the Prince. For every eligible Princess in the world is being presented for his possible selection to become his Queen. The first Princess, from Hungary, dances a Magyar step, telling Prince Siegfried of the glories of her heritage.

Then a Spanish Princess, escorted by her four brothers, appeals to Prince Siegfried to accept her as his Queen. She dances a lovely typical Spanish role . . . very discreetly, the Queen Mother looks at the expressions on her son's face. But Siegfried seems unimpressed by every Princess presented to him.

Suddenly a Russian Princess appears. With her are her handmaidens. Their clothes are so colorful and their music is so divine. How could Siegfried possibly ignore the Russian Princess's wonderful story of her Mother Russia? Undoubtedly she is everyone's favorite . . . but Siegfried remains unimpressed.

As Siegfried sinks deeper
and deeper into
contemplation, an Italian
Princess dances before
him . . .

Then a magnificently beautiful Polish Princess tries her luck. But, alas, nothing ... nobody ... not even the Queen Mother can evoke the Prince's interest in anyone.

Suddenly, from the darkest corner of the castle . . . a place where light never reaches, a stranger enters. "Who is he?" everybody asks. "Who invited him?" There are no answers, but the Queen Mother must be hospitable to all, so she beckons the stranger forward. As he approaches, a magnificent girl follows, a Black Swan Queen, with her contingent of three Black Swan Maidens.

The newcomer, Princess Odile by name, impresses every-one with her chilling beauty. But at last Siegfried shows an interest, for she looks amazingly like Odette . . . she even dances like her.

Her escort, unrecognized by everyone, is in reality, Rothbart. The lovely Odile is his daughter.

Rothbart casts a spell over Siegfried and the Prince joins the Black Swan Odile in a wonderful dance. Siegfried is sure this Black Swan Maiden is really Odette in disguise.

Odile pretends to be as tender and loving as Odette. The bewitched Siegfried fails to see through this deception.

Seeing that she is being very successful with Prince Siegfried, the treacherous Odile begins to entrap him deeper and deeper, awaiting his invitation for her to be his Queen.

As the Prince shows his love for this charming Princess, so does the crowd. She has charmed everyone as Rothbart probably has bewitched everyone in the castle.

Finally, Odile uses the oldest spell in the world. These words have worked magic for millions of years . . . "I love you," she says. Immediately, the Prince seizes her, acting as though she is the only perfect person in the world.

Rothbart's spell has entranced everyone ... except the Queen Mother. Her love for Siegfried is so great that the spell quickly vanishes from her mind ... love conquers all. She feels intuitively that something is wrong. She tries to catch Siegfried's attention, but he is not to be stopped. He has eyes only for Odile ... he has been trapped by the love spell ... love blind.

Rothbart keeps focusing his eyes on the Prince. He tries to bring Siegfried more deeply under his spell . . . he is impatient. When will Siegfried tell Odile "I love you, too" and complete the magic phrase under which men devote their lives to their chosen? The couple become more and more enmeshed in their dance . . . they ignore everyone and everything about them.

Rothbart is certain that Siegfried is completely under the spell of false love. Soon he will propose to Odile in front of all his subjects and never be able to break his promise. Rothbart will soon control the throne and the Swan Maidens will always be his toys.

Suddenly the dance ends and Siegfried is now expected to announce his choice. Everyone already knows that Odile will be their new Queen.

Odile is triumphant. She doesn't even try to act with humility. She brazenly looks everyone straight in the eye, for Siegfried is about to make his choice.

Suddenly, Siegfried has a vision . . . he sees a heavenly white swan quivering with grief. The love spell is broken and he realizes that he has been deceived. He learns his first royal lesson. The stranger is Rothbart and Odile is his daughter. Siegfried rejects Odile!! He knows that he has almost betrayed Odette and he rushes quickly to the Swan Lake . . .

Odette is suffering . . . she is a Fallen Swan . . . she has seen everything but it was far beyond her power to warn Siegfried or to do anything against the strong magic of the Love Spell or Rothbart's curses. Prince Siegfried is broken-hearted by what he sees.

The Swan Maidens are equally distraught . . . they suffer
. . . they fall into despair. How strong are the powers of
Rothbart. They will never be freed . . . they will be in
Rothbart's power forever . . . hopeless toys of a cruel
master.

Rothbart's power over them returns in full. They line up and dance to the mysterious wishes of their invisible dancemaster, Rothbart. This time, however, their sad faces reflect lost souls . . . faces without hope.

But Rothbart knows of his failure and he calls up a terrible storm to drive Odette and the Swan Maidens out of Siegfried's view. The mist thickens and the Swan Maidens disappear.

Storm or no storm . . . mist . . . fog . . . nothing can stop true love, for love conquers all! Siegfried finds Odette. The Swan Maidens are beside themselves with joy. The Prince and Odette, the Swan Queen dance together in a dance of love and reunion.

Siegfried tells Odette that he has NOT broken his vow, though involuntarily he ALMOST betrayed their love. Now that he has found her again, even through the mist and fog, the forces of love will protect them both, and he will never lose her again.

Rothbart, the evil magician rushes into the midst of the Swan Maidens in an attempt to kill Siegfried, but Odette shields Siegfried as she risks her own life in the ultimate display of true love. Siegfried repeats his solemn vow of eternal love for Odette, and as the words are uttered, Rothbart perishes.

True love conquers all!